TONY WILLIAMSON

The Courage to Conquer

—9—

Inspiring Strategies to Be Bold,
Overcome Obstacles, and Forge
Your Fantastic Future!

Copyright ©2013 Tony Williamson.
All Rights Reserved. No part of this publication may be reproduced, stored in a retrieval system or transmitted in any form or by any means, electronic, mechanical, photocopying, recording or otherwise without the permission of author or publisher.

First published in article format by The Gleaner Company Limited

National Library of Jamaica Cataloguing-in-Publication Data
Williamson, Tony
    The courage to conquer: 9 inspiring strategies to be bold, overcome obstacles and forge your fantastic future / Tony Williamson
    p. ; cm.
Bibliography: p.

ISBN 978-976-95510-8-4 (pbk)

1. Motivation   2. Self-actualization (Psychology)
3. Success   4. Affirmations   I. Title
158   dc 23

Ordering Information
Quantity (Bulk) Sales. Special discounts are available on quantity (bulk) purchases by corporations, associations, and others.
For details, contact the publisher:
sales@minnapress.com

Executive Editor: Lena J. Rose

Copy Editor: Michelle Neita

Book Designer: Mark Steven Weinberger

Published in Kingston, Jamaica

minna PRESS

www.minnapress.com

Printed in United States of America

WHAT READERS SAY

"The pathway to personal success. Tony is a brilliant writer and articulate spokesperson for how to overcome adversity and stay optimistic despite your circumstances. Being bold is a decision and Tony communicates how every one of us can take these principles and apply them to their life. This book is worth the read and should inspire the reader to not let the day-to-day factors in life dictate their attitude towards loving others, living a life of meaning and enjoying the moment."
—G. Baker, Past President, Million Dollar Round Table (MDRT) (as posted on Amazon.com)

"This is a literary masterpiece. The inspiration is incredible! I will ensure that the advisors under my watch read it and employ the amazing strategies for sales and career success. Thank you, Tony".
—Michael Isaacs, Regional Manager, Scotia Life Insurance Company, Mandeville, Jamaica.

"A brilliant literary masterpiece with timeless wisdom for any person facing challenges. Whether you are a busy parent, a young business executive, entrepreneur, college student, or ordinary professional seeking to build a career in today's challenging world and you are seeking helpful tips or suggestions that can enable you to deal with some of the difficulties you are facing, you will find "The Courage to Conquer" to be a rather inspiring, relevant and useful book. Written with engaging stories that can relate to any field or area of pursuit, this brilliant literary masterpiece contains timeless wisdom that the reader will discover to be both simple and easy to apply."
—Newton Gabbidon, President of Intercessory Prayer Ministry International, New York City

"A must have. Totally riveting. Very good motivational stories. Tony Williamson also gives practical steps to living a more productive and rewarding life."
—Gweneth Williamson (as posted on Amazon.com)

"Sometimes in life we need a little light shed on our situation to help us move forward. The contents within these covers were like a huge spotlight illuminating my path."
—Oscar F. Rodriguez, Business Owner, Miami, FL

"Spoke to me like no other. The finest writing on forgiveness I have ever read."
—Andrew Roblin, Musician and Former Journalist, Emmaus, PA

DEDICATION

For Jean, my beloved wife;
truly the greatest inspiration of my life.

CONTENTS

Foreword	9
Preface	11
Introduction	13
STRATEGY 1: SET THE STAGE FOR SUCCESS	**17**
Understanding the Power of Thought	18
Transforming Your Life by Changing Your Thinking	21
Succeed Against the Odds	24
The Importance of Sacrifice	26
The Story of Lewis Campbell	28
Living to Give	30
Move Beyond Your Fear	33
No Growth on the Mountain Top	36
A Cow in Your Backyard	39
Deep Desire Determines Destiny	41
Take Full Responsibility for Your Life	44
Believe in Yourself	47
STRATEGY 2: DREAM A BIGGER DREAM	**51**
If You Never Dream, You Never Have a Dream Come True	52
Dare to Dream and then Become Your Dream	55
From Rags to Riches: How the Power of a Dream Affected a Son of St. Ann	58
Tapping the Unseen Ability Within	61
People Who Succeeded Against the Odds	64
Living Above Your Circumstances	66
Living the Dream…From Hospital Bed to Hospital Boss	67
How Dreaming Becomes a Creative Vision	70

STRATEGY 3: CREATE A FOOLPROOF PLAN TO SUCCEED — 73

- Goal Setting: Master Key to Turning Visions into Reality — 74
- Making the Most of Priorities — 77
- Achieving Success with a D.O.M.E. Plan: Diagnosis — 80
- Achieving Success with a D.O.M.E. Plan: Objectives — 84
- Achieving Success with a D.O.M.E. Plan: Methods — 87
- Achieving Success with a D.O.M.E. Plan: Evaluation — 90
- How a D.O.M.E. Plan Saved a Life — 93

STRATEGY 4: WORK YOUR PLAN, REACH YOUR HIGHEST POTENTIAL — 97

- Work: The Difference between the Wishbone and the Backbone — 98
- Work: Going the Extra Mile — 101

STRATEGY 5: ACHIEVE OPTIMUM PERFORMANCE IN YOUR LIFE — 105

- How to Overcome Procrastination — 106
- Taking Charge of Procrastination — 109
- Managing Time Stealers — 111
- Taming Telephone Tyranny — 115
- Visitors, Meetings and Paper — 119
- The 1440 Club: Recognise that You're a Member — 122
- The 1440 Club: Change Your Mindset — 125

STRATEGY 6: MANAGE SETBACKS FOR YOUR COMEBACK — 129

- Four Choices in Times of Trouble — 130
- Promise, Problem, Provision — 132
- When Trouble Comes — 134
- Your Results Define Who You Are — 137
- The Hidden Benefits of Failure — 140
- Wilma Rudolf — 142

STRATEGY 7: DEAL WITH YOUR PAST   145
    Getting Past Your Past   146
    The Importance of Forgiveness   149
    Forgiveness: Decision Not Emotion   152

STRATEGY 8: HARNESS THE POWER OF PERSISTENCE TO PERSEVERE   155
    The Courage to Continue   156
    Persisting in the Face of Failure   159
    The Power of Persistence   162
    Code of Persistence   164

STRATEGY 9: LEARN FROM THE HORSE'S MOUTH   167
    Redemption Song   168
    Overcoming Discouragement   171
    The Dark Times of Your Life   174
    Your Best is Yet to Come   176
    Finding Your Gift   179

SUMMARY   183
    Your Master Keys to Success   184

Author's Note   194
About the Author   195
Acknowledgements   197
Bibliography   199

THE HONOURABLE R. DANNY WILLIAMS

Foreword

Tony Williamson's ***The Courage to Conquer*** is an excellent piece of work. Tony has put together an easy to read inspirational and motivating book that should be read by every young person especially those who cannot make up their mind what to do with their lives. Indeed it is a book worth reading no matter what age you are. It is a book about living a more fulfilling life, having a more meaningful existence.

The book is a gold mine of inspirational experiences that Tony himself has lived through but even more, he has drawn on the vast knowledge he has accumulated through his extensive reading as well as his exposure to some of the best in the business and brought them together so that his readers can benefit from it all. Although Tony draws on his experiences in the Jamaican Society, it does not detract from the international appeal this book should have. If anything it enhances it.

The book provides a roadmap for success in life. It highlights and demonstrates the importance of the mind, its awesome power and how it can determine what you achieve in life. It forces us to think and to take stock of our own circumstances and to ask why not? It makes you realise that you and you alone are responsible for your own circumstances and for what you become or make of your life.

Although I am in my 80th year, and I have had a successful life and although I have lived by many of the "teachings" in the book, I was reminded over and over of the many things that helped me along the way and guided me when the seas got rough. I am grateful to Tony for this because we sometimes get carried away with our own achievements and forget what we had to do to make them a reality.

One of the things that intrigued me when reading this book was the time and trouble Tony went to in order to make it a practical tool. He did not simply lay down theories but he demonstrated how they could be used in everyday life and how they could make a real difference in your life right now. Indeed you are inspired to try the tools that he has provided. They make good sense. It is also so relevant to the times in which we live.

This book provides the motivation to succeed in any vocation as well as the practical tools to achieve your goal. I do hope that all those who read this book will experience a change in their lives and be inspired to fulfill their dreams of success.

—The Hon. R. D. (Danny) Williams, OJ, CD,
Hon. LL.D.(UTECH), Hon. LL.D.(UWI), JP.

TONY WILLIAMSON

Preface

Life for me in the life insurance and financial services industry has had its thrills and spills. As I was pursuing my sales career, during the 1960s and beyond, I realised that the different experiences were teaching me about the reality of life, that is, it was made up of challenges and opportunities. More importantly, as a traveler upon the earth, I needed to have "The Courage to Conquer" if I wanted to achieve my goals and dreams.

The nuggets in these pages reflect my true life experience and those of others, as we have had to muster the courage to face our fears and conquer them. Many of the circumstances that I have managed to overcome in my life taught me that growth does not take place on the mountain top but in the valley. This is a conviction that I have spoken passionately about, and have used to help influence and inspire sales representatives under my watch as well as many other people. This, I humbly believe, has helped many to realise their potential.

I am heartened by one of the greatest conquerors of our time, the indefatigable and indomitable South African anti-apartheid revolutionary and politician, Nelson Rolihlahla Mandela. He did not settle for 'the comfortable' but spent twenty-seven grueling years in prison as he fought for the freedom of his people through the abolition of 'apartheid'. Mandela had courage, and he conquered!

The following question and guided response from practical and notable Bible teacher, Dr. Charles F. Stanley, have served me well. I have had to go through my fair share of gripping fear and failure causing me to fall flat on my face; but with a change in mindset and courage was able to rise again and again. Like him, I say to you:

When you face a hardship in life, is fear the first emotion you feel? It doesn't have to be. We can respond in faith, regardless of our circumstances. Remember, courage isn't just an attitude of toughness or determination. It is a quality of mind and spirit that enables us to meet the challenges of life with peace."[1]

Stanley further reminds us that no one chooses to go through times of pain and sorrow in life; but we can choose our response. After all, it's not what happens to us that is important; it is how we deal with what has happened that is of real importance. My view is that in the face of obstacles, we can decide to run around them, jump on top of them or jump over them. In so doing, we would have demonstrated the courage to conquer while developing into strong men and women and leaving an impact on the lives of our fellows.

In the stories you are about to read, I have made every effort to be accurate and true to the facts. It may happen, however, that despite my efforts of fidelity to the facts, my human fallibility may have trumped the reality, unknown to me. For such, I apologise in advance.

As these chapters were originally written for *The Gleaner* as a weekly column, you will find some repetition, although my editors have done their best to eliminate them.

My desire is that while you are reading each story, each quote, each thought and each experience that I was able to share in writing, you'll be filled with the courage to conquer the things you never dreamed possible. May you be prepared to meet the growth opportunities that come out of the hardships that life is throwing at you, and may you continually stretch yourself to climb the ladder of success while defeating fear and opening doors you would never have imagined.

Happy hunting!

—Tony Williamson
December 2013

[1] www.intouch.org

INTRODUCTION

Unleashing the Power Within You

What lies behind us and what lies before us are small matters compared to what lies within us. —RALPH WALDO EMERSON

The vast majority of persons in this world are living from a small fraction of their true potential, the innate ability to achieve greatness. If you look around you, 5 percent of persons are leaders. They stand out. They cut a new path. They have a vision, they influence the way people think, and they rise to the top of their chosen fields. Ninety-five percent of people are followers, "marching," as Rev. Dr. Martin Luther King Jr. puts it, "to the rhythmic drumbeat of the status quo." They do not cause things to happen; they sit by and watch things happen. In fact some even do not know what happened!

The popular colloquialism, *Nutten na gwan fi mi,* expresses a deep symptom of a lost generation, hopeless recipients of time's vicissitudes, submissive victims of life's turbulent seas, tossed about like flotsam and jetsam, without purpose, without passion, without pursuit.

Are you one of these people, living from hand to mouth, from pay cheque to pay cheque, waiting on that elusive promotion that never seems to come, waiting on that "break"? These are the people in the 95 percent.

They are followers, but more sadly, they are completely ignorant of the power within them, for if they understood what Ralph Waldo Emerson (in the above quote) meant, they would change their circumstances, make a 180-degree turn in life and rise to fabulous success, wealth, prosperity and fulfillment.

For the last forty-seven years I have studied the lives of successful men and women. I have interviewed them, watched them fall and rise again, heard their stories, and seen them fulfill their dreams, watched as they overcame deep sorrow and shattering adversity—only to rise again like the Phoenix from the ashes of temporary defeat.

What is it that they have, that we do not have? Are they more learned than we?

No, for the world is full of educated derelicts.

What they have is what we all have, a power within us, a force so great it caused Napoleon to smash his enemies and create an empire.

It caused the boy whose feet were so badly burnt, they said he would never walk again, to become a world class athlete.

It caused the great Ludwig van Beethoven to create the breathtaking, majestic Ninth Symphony, which greeted the world on May 7, 1874. What was remarkable about this great symphony is that Beethoven was stone deaf by the time he finished composing it and could not hear a note of his magnum opus, a work which is said to have had perhaps the greatest impact on Western Music. At the conclusion of the opening concert in Vienna, Beethoven remained unaware of the audience's thunderous applause until alto soloist Caroline Unger turned him around to face the hall.

Nor is blindness a barrier; John Milton wrote *Paradise Lost* while totally blind and Ray Charles went blind at six, only to rise to legendary fame.

What is the power within Portia Simpson Miller that caused her to rise, as she put it, "from the bowels of the working class", to the pinnacle of state power, smashing through the testosterone-charged barriers of male political dominance to become the first female prime minister of Jamaica?

Was it some divine spark within Joan Duncan which led her to create the vision of a uniquely tantalizing "unconditional love" for JMMB?

How did Muhammad "Cassius Clay" Ali, a stripling of a youngster, defeat the "unbeatable" Sonny Liston? How has Tiger Woods swept aside the history of black non-involvement in American golf to now bestride the sport like a Colossus?

And what was within Danny Williams, who started at an early age to sell cigarettes, which made him become arguably the greatest life insurance man of my generation. What led him to create Life of Jamaica at that time? The fact is that Danny saw an opportunity and in partnership with North American Life founded a local company, Life of Jamaica on June 1, 1970. What is more, encouraged by then finance minister, the Honourable Edward Seaga, that was the catalyst that propelled other foreign companies to localise their operations and thus ensuring that Jamaica has control over its life insurance industry.

In this book, you will learn their secrets and the secrets of other great men and women, for they will show you unmistakably how to unleash the power within you, for what lies behind you and what lies before you are indeed small matters compared to what lies within you.

Strategy 1
SET THE STAGE FOR SUCCESS

STRATEGY 1

Understanding the Power of Thought

Both poverty and riches are the offspring of thought.
—NAPOLEON HILL

The secret of unleashing the vast powers within you is the ability to unlock the immeasurable powers of the mind. Most people who are wealthy today were not born rich; they achieved their wealth through a process of thinking. Success in life is not placed upon your head like a crown inherited in a line of royalty. Success is the offspring of thought. But so is failure. Both failure and success are children of the mind, and so are poverty and wealth. It does not matter how many times you failed, or how often you went bankrupt; your thought processes can lead you again to rise from failure to success, from bankruptcy to riches, from sickness to health, from a shattered marriage to conjugal happiness.

The Bible says, "As [a man] thinketh in his heart, so is he" (Prov. 23:7). This means that we are in essence what we think, just as we are in health what we eat, except that the mind has a far more powerful influence in your life than food on the body.

Your mind is not only the steering wheel of your car, the rudder of your ship, but it is simultaneously the engine of your vehicle, the thrust of your rocket. Your body is subject to your mind. W. Clement Stone was right when he said, "You are a mind with a body". The thoughts you think are powerful, life-directing and life-transforming. They can heal or hurt. They build up or tear down. They have powerful, transcendental, long-term effects on your life. Thinking is your greatest gift, and it has the most profound influence on your life. The single most important thing that Marcus Garvey did for us was to inspire us to think; to alter our state of being by altering our state of mind.

Radio talk shows have revolutionised the thinking process of the average Jamaican. Our government must be commended on the freedom of speech it allows. You may criticise the late Wilmot Perkins as much as you like, but Perkins was doing for the common man what Garvey did for diminished Blacks—he forced us to think. Perkins was fearlessly iconoclastic and you could never assume which position he was likely to take. He was a thinker, and whether right or wrong, his conclusions came out of the searching, searing, surprising and sometimes savage questions that took the unprepared, unwary caller off guard, disarming him. If Perkins did nothing else, he taught you to think for yourself.

Thinking takes place every second of your conscious life. It drives decision-making. The car you drive, the chair in your living room, the corner on which you sit or stand to sell fruits or the newspaper, the person you married, the radio station which you tune into, the job you now have—all were FIRST ideas in the mind. Your physical circumstances are largely an expression of the thoughts of your mind. Your thoughts drive you, they direct you, and they lead you to forgiveness or revenge, to love or to hate, to sickness or to health, to poverty or to riches.

WHAT YOU THINK UPON GROWS WITHIN YOU.

Whatever you allow yourself to think about persistently becomes big in your life. This is true whether your thoughts are good or evil. As the thing grows and magnifies itself in your life, it drives you relentlessly, inexorably toward the achievement of that thing. Your persistent thoughts become self-fulfilling, a creative vision, for good or ill. A creative vision can be good—like the Mahatma Ghandi's vision of an independent India, like Nelson Mandela's vision of a just South Africa for all, like Martin Luther King's, "I Have A Dream" vision of racial equality. Persistent thoughts can also yield nightmares of destructive achievement, like Hitler's vision of a super race of Aryans, resulting in the destruction of six million Jews, or Jim Jones' suicidal implosion in the jungles of Guyana.

But can you control your thoughts? Can you decide what you think? Find out as you read the ensuing chapters.

STRATEGY 1

Transforming Your Life by Changing Your Thinking

The greatest discovery of my generation is that human beings can alter their lives by altering their attitudes of mind. We need only to act as if the thing in question were real and it will become infallibly real by growing in such a connection in your life that it will become real. —WILLIAM JAMES

In October 1970, I was a young life insurance salesman and, in plying my trade, I met a couple who were to become close friends of my family and me. The couple were expatriates from New Zealand, and the husband, Errol, was an information technology specialist hired by Alcan at its Kirkvine Works.

My wife Jean had become particularly close to Margie, Errol's wife. The two young wives had much in common as they compared notes on raising their children and coping with their irascible, "Type A" husbands.

The time came when Errol's contract ended and they returned to New Zealand. Sometime after, we received a telephone call that shocked and distressed us. Margie had been diagnosed with a particularly virulent form of cancer and was given only three months to live.

Distraught, Jean took the earliest available flight to Auckland and then an internal flight to Palmerston North where Margie lived. She wanted to spend some time with her dear friend before she died. After a few days Jean called me and said: "Hon, I am truly amazed at what I am seeing here. I came here to cheer up Margie, but she is cheering me up. She refuses to accept a sentence of death by a doctor's diagnosis of terminal cancer. She is saying 'This cancer will not defeat me. I will defeat it.' Margie is repeating this aloud to herself and to all the household day in, day out." But Margie did something else. She changed her diet to raw food and nuts and moved away from Palmerston North to shield herself from any possible negative influences. She took only her diet and her Bible, and she believed intensely that through prayer, a positive mental attitude, and a change in her eating habits, she would whip cancer.

I tell Margie's story wherever I speak motivationally, all around the world, and I end her story this way: "Ladies and gentlemen, sadly, Margie did not make it. She lost the battle with cancer, but guess what? She lost it twenty years later!" Not only did the cancer go into remission, Margie's best years were to come. The three months she was given to live became twenty years, and she returned to Jamaica over that time to share her story, how by changing her thinking she extended her life.

It was not until I became an emergency medical technician that I began to hear from doctors how critical a role the mind plays in recovery—or non-recovery. Several critical care doctors have told me that their patients who have a will to survive, who fight mentally, make remarkable recoveries while others who give up simply die. The mind does affect the body, and psychosomatic illnesses are well known.

If changing your thinking can affect your body, what can it do for your career or your marriage? What can it do for your constant indebtedness or your maxed out credit cards; for your spiritual life; your hand-to-mouth existence? The more you think about affliction, sickness and disease, the worse it will become. The more you think of yourself as healthy and vivacious, the more you will achieve it, for what you think upon grows, magnifying itself in your life. The same principle applies to your finances.

The more you dwell mentally upon poverty, hard times and difficult circumstances, the more these things manifest themselves in your life. On the other hand by focusing on prosperity and abundance, you can move yourself from "rags to riches".

STRATEGY 1

Succeed Against the Odds

The heights by great men reached and kept were not attained by sudden flight, but they, while their companions slept, were toiling upwards in the night.—HENRY WADSWORTH LONGFELLOW

If you have an intense, implacable and burning desire to succeed, you will succeed despite the odds against you. The people who are successful today, the rich and famous, the super achievers, were not born with the proverbial gold spoon in their mouths. Many, perhaps most, had to overcome staggering odds, obstacles and difficulties to be where they are today. You may see them living in Beverley Hills, or driving a Lexus or Mercedes Benz, but many of these same people were born in ordinary circumstances, some in deep poverty. Others had physical disabilities and faced seemingly insurmountable obstacles. Some were abused as children, others were abandoned. Some dropped out of school—many referred to as 'dunces'—but went on to succeed in life.

  I once attended a function in which the late Paul Geddes, the Red Stripe Beer mogul and multi-millionaire was being honoured. The guest speaker of the evening made an interesting observation in his speech. He said it was not unusual that while at school there were always some people who came in the bottom five percent of the class. But here's the interesting thing: the bottom five percent often went on in life to employ the top five percent! When Paul Geddes got up to speak and to accept his award, I'll never forget what he said, "Ladies and gentlemen", he shyly remarked, "I was one of those in the bottom five percent of class."

The fact is that life deals each of us a certain hand. But it is not the hand that life deals you that is important. What is REALLY important is how you play your cards. It's not the wind that blows, it's the set of the sail. Your brain, your imagination, your will to succeed is what will take you from failure to success. You do not need a university degree (I have nothing against a university degree). You do not need to have been born in a wealthy family. You do not need to be white, brown, black or yellow. All you need is an intense desire to succeed, an uncompromising belief in yourself and your potential, and a way to see obstacles as stepping stones to success. Of course, hard work is what turns potential to achievement.

STRATEGY 1

The Importance of Sacrifice

Verily, verily, I say unto you, except a corn of wheat fall into the ground and die, it abideth alone, but if it die, it bringeth forth much fruit.—THE HOLY BIBLE, KJV, JOHN 12:24

As a young man, I was fascinated by success. I asked myself: "Why do some people succeed and the vast majority of persons simply endure an existence? Why do leaders emerge and leave the majority marching to the rhythmic drumbeat of the status quo?" As I studied the biographies of successful men and women, the answer came to me: They made a sacrifice.

Every successful person, every major accomplishment, every breathtaking achievement was FIRST made a reality by a sacrifice. So many wealthy and successful people today can point to a specific sacrifice they made, or a particular time period during which they deliberately endured hardship to achieve a goal.

DEATH BEFORE LIFE

Great achievers, life's heroes and the super wealthy all share a common experience. They had to undergo a period that was so testing, so lonely, and so difficult, it felt like death. But it was during that period of "death" that their characters were fashioned. Many of us today were privileged to receive a good education. Our parents were not rich, but they made a sacrifice. Instead of making one more dress, mom saved the money in her thread bag—here a little, there a little, going without life's luxuries so that her children would receive the best education, something which they perhaps did not receive themselves. Some of these parents did not live long enough to see us thrive, but their selfless sacrifice is responsible for whatever measure of success we enjoy today.

One of the major causes of poverty is a failure to understand that a sacrifice must precede wealth. There is a sowing before a reaping. There is an accumulation phase before a consumption phase. The more sacrifice you make in saving and investing, the wealthier you eventually become.

I know of a fabulously wealthy person so I asked him to tell me his story. He related a remarkable account of a business idea that was so strong in his mind that he and his wife sold everything they possessed to capitalise that business. Then they continued the sacrifice by living very thriftily, cutting all unnecessary expenses, and watching their business as it grew. Today, he is a wealthy man, but looks back pensively to the time he sold all he had, in order to invest in his business idea.

In the year 2007, on a trip to Africa, I met a remarkable couple, Moses and Juliet Klinogo. Reflecting on a time when he was dirt poor, Moses recounted how he was not able to afford a pair of shoes. He was also deep in debt. While in the darkness of despair, he was given an opportunity with a company with which I am associated. The opportunity was in network marketing. He made a sacrifice to sell three pairs of his trousers to buy products. Today, he earns in excess of US$1 million per year from his base in Accra, Ghana. Moses says, "We knew all we needed was the determination to be successful. Today, we are reaping the rewards of taking that attitude from early on."

What do you need to do to achieve your breakthrough? What about cutting up those credit cards, making a sacrifice to come out of debt? This may well be the start of a new, exciting and dynamic life.

STRATEGY 1

The Story of Lewis Campbell

Success seems to be connected with action.
Successful people keep moving.
They make mistakes but don't quit. —CONRAD HILTON

At age nine, Lewis Campbell almost lost his life by drowning. He fell into a St. Ann water tank and, unable to swim, he went down twice to the bottom. He was determined not to go down the third time because "three strikes, you're out!" On the way up the second time, he remembered someone saying that if you flail your arms you would stay afloat. So he pulled his cap over his face, flailed his arms and kept on top of the water until someone pulled him out.

      He entered the life insurance industry in 1976, but he enjoyed only average success. He then went to work as general manager for a Kingston firm, but left after two years to pursue his dream of running his own business. His business was trucking, but the treacherous Mt. Rosser and the curvaceous hills of St. Ann conspired against him. His business crashed and burned and he hit the bottom with a thud. Broke and deep in debt, he again flailed his arms and started to swim for his life. He knocked on doors, he sent resumes, and he answered 'Wanted' ads. Nothing! But he kept on. He had a wife and three children and, if the truth be told, at times they had little in the house to eat.

Finally, National Cash Register (NCR) offered him a job as one of their marketing managers. Lewis is a persuasive talker with an analytical mind. The two talents began to propel him again, upward, to fresh air. But as he was reaching the top of his game, NCR signaled its intention to close its doors in Jamaica. A door of hope was about to slam shut. Instead of fearing joblessness and the danger of another period of unemployment, Lewis analysed the situation. During his time at NCR he had seen the huge problems their clients were facing with power problems and an unreliable public electricity service. Peoples' computers were going ballistic. Then it hit him: "One man's problem is another man's opportunity. If I can provide people with reliable, uninterrupted power, I'm gone clear!" With nothing but courage in his heart, he approached the mighty Toshiba Industrial Corporation, Houston, Texas and somehow convinced them to give him a franchise and credit.

Today, Lewis sits as CEO of Electronic Power Solutions Limited (EPSOL), a multimillion dollar business for Power Quality Products and Services. Once gasping for air, Lewis is now a leader in his field. Says Lewis, "One thing I can tell you, when one door closes, a window opens up somewhere else for you. The road to the top is not easy, but when you are at the top you can eat better. Never give up if you fail at first. Keep trying, and if you stumble, fall on your back so you can look up and see the blue sky. For the sky not only gives you hope, the sky is the limit of your potential."

STRATEGY 1

Living to Give

Give, and you will receive, your gift will return to you
in full-pressed down, shaken together to make room for more,
running over and poured back into your lap. The amount you give
will determine the amount you get back. —THE HOLY BIBLE, NLT, LUKE 6:38

Everything that is living is giving. The sun gives its light, the birds give their song, the flowers give their nectar, and the dog gives its unconditional love. The only thing that does not give is something that is dead. Giving is one of the pivotal features of a living thing. If everything that is living is giving, then if you are not giving, you know your problem.

I have engaged myself over the last forty years in a study of successful and wealthy men and women. I can tell you with unshakeable certainty that wealthy people have certain common features that set them apart from the crowd. They are big dreamers. They are goal-oriented. They use failure as an opportunity to begin again more intelligently. They take responsibility for their actions—they don't blame others. But one particular interesting commonality is that, with few exceptions, they are generous givers. And the more they give, the more they seem to receive.

There are many immutable laws that govern our space-time world. Sir Isaac Newton defined some laws of physics. One of these said, "To every action there is always an equal and opposite or contrary, reaction". This law functions with, for example, a jet plane. The jet blasts backward propelling the aircraft forward. This law has also a spiritual, indefinable truth about it. The Bible says, "Whatever a man sows that shall he also reap". The law of giving falls into this truthful, though almost inexplicable, quality, "Give, and you will receive". The laws of the universe come together to ensure that a giver always receives.

On the other hand, meanness and stinginess is a soul-shriveling attitude. The saddest spectacle on earth is that of a mean man. His bank account may be large, but his soul is small, pitiful and bankrupt.

HOW, WHEN AND WHAT TO GIVE

One of the discoveries I have made about generous givers who are now wealthy is that they were givers before they became wealthy. These people did not wait until wealth came their way in order to give. They gave to others sacrificially, and wealth came. They then continued to give.

One of the world's richest men is Bill Gates. He is also one of the world's biggest givers. Jamaica's billionaire, Michael Lee-Chin is known for his incredible generosity. These people will become richer and richer as they give more and more away because, "for every action there is an equal and opposite reaction".

You do not have to give cash. You can give of your time in community service, you can teach a literacy class, mentor a young person or give freely of the blessings with which you have been blessed. This is giving. You can also give financially—to the poor, the oppressed, and the hungry. You could pay for someone's books, school fees or hospital bill.

MOTIVE FOR GIVING

Although you will receive as you give, your motive in giving should be love of your fellowman—not giving to receive. You will receive anyway, but love must drive your giving.

THE DEAD SEA

Some years ago I was in Israel and visited the Dead Sea. There is no life in this sea. It is briny and salty in the extreme. But not far from the Dead

Sea was the Sea of Galilee, alive and full of fish and living creatures. Both the Sea of Galilee and the Dead Sea have one thing in common. They are both recipients of water from the River Jordan. But there is one big difference; the Sea of Galilee receives water from Jordan in the north and lets out the same water in the south. It receives on one side and gives back on the other side.

The Dead Sea receives the same water but has no outlet for it. It receives but does not give. It is dead—suffocated by its inability to release stagnant water. Based on these observations, I have formed the opinion, "You keep what you give; you lose what you hoard".

STRATEGY 1

Move Beyond Your Fear

Come to the edge, He said.
They said: We are afraid.
Come to the edge, He said.
They came. He pushed them,
And they flew. —GUILLAUME APOLLINAIRE

It is impossible with finite minds to know how many dreams were unfulfilled, how many ideas were stillborn, how many great and transcendental feats were never accomplished because of fear. Recently, a friend and I were driving past a cemetery and he remarked, "You know, that place is the richest plot of land."

"What do you mean?" I asked him. He replied, "It is filled with unwritten books, plans that were never achieved, scientific ideas that were never patented, cures for sicknesses that were never revealed. People died with these ideas and for fear of failure, never acted upon them."

Millions have never achieved their goals because they feared the consequences of attempting them. We receive so many creative ideas, so many thoughts that could revolutionise our lives, transform poverty into wealth, sickness into health, sorrow into joy, and yet, because of fear, we never venture out of our comfort zone to attempt these things.

Fear is an interesting thing. It is a necessary component of life. Not all fear is bad. Fear causes you to pause to assess danger and to take the necessary steps to minimise risk. Fear should also prevent someone from swimming across a crocodile infested river, but it should not prevent such a person from crossing the river at all. If you need to get to the other side, you choose to ride in a boat. Fear becomes crippling and debilitating when, even though you have access to a boat, the fear of crocodiles prevents you from crossing the river at all.

The paradox of fear is that it can become a phobia, a crippling, disabling part of one's life; something that acts as a damper to any new idea, any venture.

There are people who trap themselves in dead-end jobs, not even venturing to send out a resume. They want another job, but they fear leaving the one they have. They fear risk. But life is a risk. Every successful venture was once a risk. There is a risk of failure, but there is the opportunity to succeed. It is impossible to achieve the success without taking the risk. Frederick Wilcox was right, "Progress always involves risk. You can't steal second base and keep your foot on first."

FEEL THE FEAR, AND DO IT ANYWAY

Author Susan Jeffers suggests that we feel the fear and do it anyway. Clearly, she could not be saying that we should act recklessly or irresponsibly. She is recognizing the fact that fear is natural. Whenever you begin a new venture, start a new project, enter a new job, confront an unusual situation, there is fear, and this is where there is a dividing line between successful people and those who do not achieve their goals. Successful people feel the fear like the rest of us, but it does not prevent them from doing the things that they want to do, or have to do. High achievers sense the fear we all sense, but they plunge ahead because the reward to be gained is a stronger motivation than the fear they feel. If your motivation is stronger than your fear, you will take action. I certainly would not swim across a crocodile infested river, but if my grandchild fell in the river, I'd be in the water in a flash. The reward of saving that child is greater than the fear of crocodiles.

TAKING STOCK

Before you fail to act because of fear, do this simple exercise. Get a blank sheet of paper and draw a line down the middle. On the left, write the word FOR. On the right, place the word AGAINST. Proceed to list all the reasons you should go ahead with your proposal or plan. On the other side, list all the reasons you should not. Usually, the decision is plain before your eyes with this simple decision-making tool.

In the final analysis, what Bob Proctor said is food for thought: "We come this way but once. We can tiptoe through life and hope that we get to death without being too badly bruised, or we can live a full, complete life achieving our goals and realizing our wildest dreams."

STRATEGY 1

No Growth on the Mountain Top

Sweet are the uses of adversity, which, like the toad,
ugly and venomous, wears yet a precious jewel in his head.
—WILLIAM SHAKESPEARE

Dreaming is only the beginning of a journey to success. Fulfilling the dream is often very challenging, with many, successful people having to pay a heavy price for the reward. When you see successful people driving their Lexuses, and Mercedes Benzes, living in Beverley Hills or Cherry Gardens, flying first class and making the news, don't envy them. For many have endured excruciating agony, sleepless nights, faced and staved off bankruptcies, endured "bad mouthing", sweated over the monthly payroll, and yet, triumphed. The people who have endured trials and tribulation, who have experienced pain and suffering and come through, are people of strong character—men and women whose spirits and minds have been moulded in the fire of trials.

But why, however, does life deal hard times to people? Why not just be wafted through life on a satin pillow of success? The fact is that success would most likely destroy many people who had no experience of defeat and difficulty. It's the same with money. Money quickly gained or inherited, money won through a lottery, is often just as quickly lost by people who never had to pay a price for it, people whose characters are like marshmallows rather than steel.

Some years ago my wife and I took a trip over a section of the Canadian Rockies. We boarded a cable car and were transported slowly over the beautiful scenery. In the valley where we boarded the cable car, there was lush vegetation, huge trees, each rivaling the other as to how high it could grow. It was a virtual jungle. As we went higher and higher in the cable car however, we noticed that there were fewer and fewer trees, less and less vegetation.

When we finally reached the snow covered mountain top, the scene was spectacular, breathtaking. The air was crisp and clean, you could see for miles around. One had the feeling of ecstasy, of power, of wonder at nature. But we noticed something else—there was no vegetation, no trees, and no growth at the mountain top.

It was then that it struck me, "This is the journey of life", I thought to myself, "When you reach the top, the air is rare, the sights are great, but there is no growth there." It was in the valley where we boarded the cable car, that growth was fierce. Competition forced each tree to grow higher and higher to reach its share of the sunlight. The valley was hot and difficult, but that is where the growth took place, not at the top.

The valley in your life represents the adversity and trials you now face. It is during these trials that you grow, not when you reach the top, for life is like a fruit; when you're green you grow, when you're ripe you rot. To prevent "rot", when you reach the top, do not see it as a final stop. View success as a journey, not a destination.

In my life I have watched people acquire power or wealth or both. But sadly, I saw some of them change to arrogant, pompous and impatient people who let power and wealth dominate their thinking. They run roughshod over people. If they are employers, they brook no compromise, they tolerate no dissention. Their philosophy: "It's my way or the highway." These people have either forgotten the valley or have not learned from it. But life, the great leveler of men, tends to balance their arrogance with humbling experiences until they learn that humility is a sign of greatness.

There is a principle of success which holds true every time: promise, problem, provision. The promise is your dream, and the provision, your reward. But you never gain the provision without successfully negotiating the problem. There are no exceptions to this rule.

Promise, problem, provision; the principle never fails. If you conquer the problem, you will walk humbly. Until you learn to handle success, life places you back into the problem for as long as it takes to straighten you out. It took forty years in the backside of the desert to straighten Moses out. Let's hope it takes less time with you and me.

STRATEGY 1

A Cow In Your Backyard

I can see the cattle on a thousand hills, as beautiful
as they are far away. I must go and fetch me some cattle.
Oh, how I wish I had a cow in my backyard!
—TONY WILLIAMSON

In a very real sense, man has been cursed by the concept of the "grass being greener on the other side." Multiplied thousands across the ages have unknowingly left riches in their own backyard for that elusive, dream of wealth on the other side. If the truth be told, many times your success, potential wealth, self-actualisation and fulfillment can be found exactly where you are now, not in the "greener pastures" on the other side. Let me tell you a true story that will illustrate this point. This amazing story was told in lecture form thousands of times by Dr. Russell Conwell, founder of Temple University.

THE STORY OF LAMAR

Years ago, when the first diamonds were being discovered in Africa, diamond fever spread like wildfire across the continent. Men were becoming fabulously wealthy overnight as they mined the earth for the precious stone. It appeared almost limitless across Africa.

While all of this was happening, Lamar was a young farmer in central Africa, scratching out a miserable existence on his farm. As he heard the stories of the great diamonds and the wealth they instantly brought, he became increasingly dissatisfied with his own situation. One day he could bear it no more. His overpowering desire for instant wealth drove him to impulsively sell his farm, pack a few essentials and leave his family in search of those magnificent diamonds. Instant wealth was his for the taking.

His search was long, painful, arduous and debilitating. He wandered across Africa, fighting wild beasts and insects, sleeping under the stars, wet from rain, hot from the sun. Day after day Lamar searched, week after week, month after month, but found no diamonds. He became sick, penniless, hungry, exhausted and discouraged. Finally, he concluded that there was nothing more to live for. He threw himself in a river and drowned.

Meanwhile, back on the farm that Lamar had impulsively sold, the new owner was farming, working the soil. One day, this new farmer came across a large unusual stone in a small creek that ran across the farm. The farmer thought it a strange object but, unaware of what it was, brought it into his farmhouse and placed it on the fireplace mantle as a curio.

Sometime later, a visitor came to the farmer's house and noticed the unusual stone. He quickly grasped the stone and shouted excitedly. "Do you know this is a diamond? It is one of the largest diamonds I've ever seen!" Upon further investigation they discovered that the entire farm was covered with large, magnificent diamonds. As a matter of fact, this farm turned out to be one of the richest and most productive diamond mines in the world, and the farmer became one of Africa's wealthiest men.

What can we learn from this true story? Well, the cow you seek on the mountain is probably already in your own backyard, if you look closely. Your mind is a diamond mine. Your thinking power is invaluable. Even if you are broke now, never say you have nothing, for if you have your imagination you have everything. Before you pull up roots and "seek another job," ask yourself what diamonds might be hidden in your own job. Often great riches are "hidden in plain sight". Sometimes a change is what you need, but not before you have carefully explored the potential in your present situation. And, by the way, be careful how you lust after the other man's green grass, because his grass may be green because it is growing over his septic tank.

STRATEGY 1

Deep Desire Determines Destiny

Some of us seem to accept the fatalistic position...
that the Creator accorded to us a certain position
and condition and therefore there is no need trying
to be otherwise. —MARCUS GARVEY

Destiny is not a matter of chance, it is a matter of choice.
—WILLIAM JENNINGS BRYAN

Some years ago I was one of the main platform speakers at a large conference of life insurance and financial advisors in the Far East. I cannot now recall what I spoke on, but interestingly, I recall in vivid detail what the Taiwanese speaker dealt with as his topic. He spoke on desire which, he said, was the sine qua non of success. What graphically etched his speech in my mind was a story he told about the type of desire that brings success. Here is the story:

> There was once an old, wise, African man who lived on a mountainside. Below the mountain, not far from his small hut, was a lake which glistened and shimmered under the hot African sun. The wisdom of this elder was legendary. Solomonic. People would beat a steady path to his humble

cottage, seeking his wise advice and counsel. The sage spent hours in front of his small hut, and as he counseled many, he rocked back and forth in an old rocking chair. When he was not giving advice, he spent hours on end in solitary pensiveness in that rocking chair.

One day, a young tribal warrior came to see him. He stood erect and proud, a spear in his hand, as the ivory rings on each earlobe seemed to signal a warrior destined for greatness.

"How may I assist you?" said the elder, graciously.

The young warrior replied, "I am from a distant village, but I have heard of your great wisdom. I have traveled many days to see you, for the great elders of my tribe have told me that you can give me the secret of happiness and success."

The old man listened intently, but said not a word. He looked down at the ground for several moments then, as if carrying the weight of future generations on his octogenarian shoulders, he rose slowly. He looked the young warrior intently in the eye and still, with not a word uttered, he grasped the boy's hand and led him on the path down to the gleaming lake. Although obviously puzzled, the young warrior followed the wordless elder. Soon they reached the lake but, surprisingly, the elder kept walking with the boy. Out into the water the old man led the boy, getting deeper and deeper with each step. Soon the water was at the boy's knees, then the further out they walked, the higher the water rose, to the boy's waist, to his chest, but still the old man kept walking. Now the water was at his chin, and finally, the lad was totally submerged.

The old man stopped and waited—15 seconds, 30 seconds, 45 seconds. Carbon dioxide began to fill the boy's system and at 60 seconds the automatic cerebral processes that override the will not to breathe were about to kick in when, with his lungs at the point of bursting, the old man turned him around and his head shot out of the water, gasping for life-giving oxygen.

They walked back to the hut in silence and after some agonizing minutes, the old man asked the young warrior, "Young man, when you were under water, what was it that you desired most?" Angrily, the boy replied, "Why, I was desperate for air. I was about to drown. I wanted to breathe, you old idiot."

Then the wise man spoke these words: "My son, when you want happiness and success in life as badly as you wanted to breathe, you will have found the secret."

What do you desire in life? When you desire it to the point where you can taste it, touch it, smell it, see it and hear it, it will be yours.

Indeed, deep desire determines destiny.

STRATEGY 1

Take Full Responsibility for Your Life

People are always blaming their circumstances for what they are. I don't believe in circumstances. The people who get on in this world are those who get up and look for the circumstances they want—and if they can't find them, they make them.—GEORGE BERNARD SHAW

Jim Rohn, the American business philosopher says, "You must take personal responsibility. You cannot change the circumstances, the seasons or the wind, but you can change yourself".

Millions of people in the world are under a strong, debilitating and destructive delusion about life. They believe that life owes them something, that they are entitled to succeed, that other people, somewhere, somehow are responsible for filling their lives with wealth, joy and happiness. Many of these persons, blighted by this delusion, cry "Nutten na gwan fi mi." But, if the truth be told, there is only one person on the face of this earth who is responsible for your success, your happiness, your wealth, and your relationships.

That person is you.

If you want to be successful, if you desire to reverse a downward spiral in your life, if you wish to move ahead from this very moment, you must take complete responsibility for everything you are today, for all the results you produce, for the state of your health, for your debts and maxed out credit cards, for the quality of your relationships, your income, your feelings and your station in life.

Most people have the tendency to blame others for what happens to them. Children blame their parents for their outcomes, employees blame their bosses, husbands blame their wives, and citizens blame the government. If we are depressed, we blame the weather. If our savings are eroded by inflation we blame the economy. If we have no money, we blame the system. We tend to look outside of ourselves to find the reasons for our failures instead of putting up a mirror in front of our face and saying, "Here is the REAL problem. I am looking at him."

The starting point of genuine success in life—and it can start today—is to say to yourself with honesty and acceptance, "As of today, I take one hundred percent responsibility for my life. I will not look outside of myself for success or failure. If it's going to be, it's up to me". Once you can say that and truly mean it, you have made a major change in your life and started on the high road of personal achievement. Jack Canfield puts it this way, "… you create everything that happens to you. It means you understand that you are the cause of all of your experience. If you want to be really successful… then you will have to give up blaming and complaining, and take total responsibility for your life."

EXCUSITIS

The first step in taking full responsibility for your life is to abandon the habit of making excuses. Excuses are the common denominator of failures in life—"The devil made me do it."

George Washington Carver said, "Ninety-nine percent of all failures come from people who have a habit of making excuses." Excuses are the comfort of fools and the spawning ground for under-achievement. If you want an example of this, ask habitually late people why they are late. "The traffic was heavy". But the responsible answer might be, "I left home late." "I am late because my wife had to go to the pharmacy". "The alarm did not go off this morning". These are all examples of excusitis and you could multiply these by thousands—to take care of your debts, your divorce, your diabetes, your income, your failure to be promoted at work.

Going forward, you must draw a line in the sand and say, "Enough is enough, the past has passed. I choose to go forward. I will accept total responsibility. I will succeed. This is a new day."

My friend, circumstances are not the problem. Whatever your circumstances now, there are thousands of persons who have faced similar circumstances, and have succeeded. If they could do it, so can you.

STRATEGY 1

Believe in Yourself

Belief kill, an belief cure. —JAMAICAN PROVERB

Bestselling author, Max Lucado, made a statement which caught my eye, and is the basis of this section. He said, "You weren't an accident. You weren't mass produced. You aren't an assembly-line product. You were deliberately planned, specifically gifted, and lovingly positioned on the Earth by the Master Craftsman."

A most important element in life's success is the importance of believing in yourself. Many people fail to achieve their full potential because they concentrate their belief on "I can't" instead of "I can". Call it what you will—self-esteem, a right attitude or positive thinking, if you do not believe, you will not achieve. There is a purpose to your life, and the Master Craftsman has given you the inner resources, the talents, the abilities to achieve your goals and to fulfill your dreams.

DAMAGE FROM OUR CHILDHOOD

We come into this world with only two fears, scientists tell us—the fear of falling and the fear of loud noises. Everything else we now fear was instilled in us by our parents, our society, our relationships and our experience. In fact, many people have to overcome serious mental damage done to them by their parents or caregivers when they were children; damage which they carry around today as emotional baggage. Let me be specific.

A great number of children in this country have been told by teachers, parents and caregivers that they are "dunces". Angry mothers have told their sons "Yu wutliss wretch. Yu no good. Yu just like yu puppa." As a child growing up, I was aware of the horrible, verbal, and physical abuse by a neighbour on her adopted daughter. Between physical beatings, she was told the most horrible things—that she was trash, would amount to no good, and things of that nature. The girl, a bright, winsome child was able to overcome this to become an outstanding college professor in science subjects—but not before she left that environment of abuse.

An upbringing that exposes people to false negatives—that they are dunces, no good and worthless- is the seedbed for a lack of belief in themselves as they become adults. Many verbally abusive caregivers have good intentions but let their anger at a child get the better of them. They are unaware of the power of words. They remember the highly erroneous jingle, "Sticks and stones may break my bones but words will never hurt me." Nothing could be further from the truth. Sticks and stones may damage your body. Words damage your mind, leaving emotional scars that you may carry to your grave.

FREEING YOURSELF

Bob Marley popularised Marcus Garvey's words, "Emancipate yourself from mental slavery, none but ourselves can free our minds." Here are some steps to take in overcoming fear and believing in yourself:

1. **You are destined to succeed, not to fail.** If you were told as a child that you were destined to fail, you were given false information. God made you a winner, not a loser. The Master Craftsman made you special, for a purpose, and He gave you the ability to succeed. Believe that.

2. **By a deliberate decision, you must forgive those who sowed the seeds of failure in your mind.** Say like Jesus, "Father, forgive them, for they know not what they were doing."

3. **Develop the "I can" attitude and drop the "I can't" philosophy.** Paul R. Scheele, Chairman, Learning Strategies Corporation says, "The phrase 'I can't' is the most powerful force of negation in the human psyche." Barack Obama is rewriting American political history by his mantra "Yes we can."

4. **Identifying your strengths.** We all have strengths and weaknesses. My good friend and motivational speaker, Winston Bennett, makes the point, "Don't waste your energy trying to improve your weaknesses. Manage those as best you can. Instead, maximise your strengths." Billionaire Richard Bronson is said to be dyslexic. He may not have ended up as a rocket scientist, but he concentrated on his gifting as an entrepreneur, and created Virgin Atlantic Airlines. Our own Paul Desnoes failed at school, but took over his father's business and went on with others to expand Desnoes and Geddes to become a billion-dollar empire.

5. **Forget the negatives that others say about you.** Others cannot define you. Only you can define yourself. People have no obligation to believe in you, but you have an obligation to believe in yourself. Tennis champion, Venus Williams is right, "You have to believe in yourself when no one else does. That's what makes you a winner. And always remember God made you SPECIAL."

Strategy ②
DREAM A BIGGER DREAM

STRATEGY 2

If You Never Dream, You Never Have a Dream Come True

Hold fast to your dreams, for if dreams die, then life is like a broken-winged bird that cannot fly. —LANGSTON HUGHES

Every great achievement you see today was once an impossible dream. The imagination is one of the most powerful things on earth. The song To Dream the Impossible Dream is a song we should always have in our hearts. Dream big things, impossible things! Don't tread the same old, worn out path. Go instead where there is no path, and cut a swath where others may follow.

There is no difference between the amount of neurological energy expended to think small thoughts and that required to think big thoughts. The bigger the dream, the greater the possibility! Dr. Martin Luther King, Jr. had a dream that one day, blacks would be judged not by the colour of their skin, but by the content of their character. He pronounced his famous I Have a Dream speech at a time when the darkness of segregation covered the American landscape. If he could see Barack Obama, elected President of the United States, he would smile with pride.

Every great achievement was once impossible until someone made it a reality. The V-8 engine was "impossible" until Henry Ford lived his impossible dream. Heavier-than-air machines should not be able to fly, but the jumbo jet flies today because the Wright brothers dreamed the impossible dream.

BELIEVE THE IMPOSSIBLE

Lewis Carroll's masterpiece, *Through the Looking Glass,* has a section in it that exemplifies the need to dream the impossible dream. It appears in a conversation between the queen and Alice, and it goes like this:

"I can't believe that", said Alice.

"Can't you?" the queen said pitifully. "Try again, draw a long breath, and shut your eyes."

Alice chuckled. "There's no use trying," she said. "One can't believe impossible things."

"I daresay you haven't had much practice," the queen responded. "When I was your age, I always did it for half an hour a day. Why, sometimes I've believed as many as six impossible things before breakfast."

TRY IT FOR HALF AN HOUR

It is said that everyday there is at least one thought, one idea that passes through our mind, which if acted upon, could make us multi-millionaires and fabulously successful. But we dismiss these thoughts and forget them. Here's my suggestion:

- Get up earlier, or find a quiet place where you may think and dream undisturbed. Take pen and paper, and write down the thoughts that come to your mind about success.

- How might you acquire financial wealth? Write it down.

- How can you secure a home? Write down the thoughts that come to your mind.

- See yourself as eminently successful; driving the type of car you want. If you want to be wealthy, dream of fabulous wealth. As they told us at the Million Dollar Round Table, "Dare to dream, and then become your dream."

USE YOUR IMAGINATION

Albert Einstein spoke of the imagination as one of the greatest gifts to man. He saw himself riding on a beam of light and soon he wrote the world-shattering Theory of Relativity. When the great inventor Thomas Alva Edison was asked how he explained his prolific inventiveness he replied, "It is because I never think in words; I think in pictures."

You can achieve phenomenal success if you visualise your dreams. Hold on to them. If you want something badly enough, see yourself in possession of the thing NOW, and it will be yours. There is a section of your brain known as the Reticular Activating System (RAS) that research has shown to be a force that drives you relentlessly to achieve that which you think of constantly. Anything that is thought about repeatedly passes to your subconscious and you are driven, for good or ill, to achieve that thing. Your thoughts affect your physical body and your life in general.

Dream big dreams and you will achieve big things. Dream little things, and you become your dream. And remember the timeless words of Napoleon Hill, "Whatever the mind of man can conceive and believe, it can achieve."

STRATEGY 2

Dare to Dream, and then Become Your Dream

Dream lofty dreams, and as you dream, so shall you become. Your vision is the promise of what you shall at last unveil. —JOHN RUSKIN

Dr. Benjamin Mays, president emeritus of Morehouse College, once said the following:

> It must be borne in mind that the tragedy of life does not lie in not reaching your goals, the tragedy lies in not having any goals to reach. It isn't a calamity to die with dreams unfulfilled, but it is a calamity not to dream. It is not a disaster to be unable to capture your ideals, but it is a disaster to have no ideals to capture. It is not a disgrace not to reach the stars, but it is a disgrace to have no stars to reach.

The above quotation from this outstanding scholar and educator speaks to one of the greatest truths in life. Men and women of every age, boys and girls, should have this written out and placed in their bedrooms, their offices, even their bathrooms. This applies not only to young people, but to persons of any age, even advanced age. For, dreaming is not limited by age. You can become your dream at any age. If John McCain had become president of the United States he would have lived his dream at age 71. Our own Jamaican national hero, the late Sir Alexander Bustamante became prime minister of Jamaica at age 78! I read recently of an elderly lady who at age 84 graduated from an American university.

Here are two things you must bear in mind: if you never dream, you never have a dream come true. The second thing is this: The only dreamless sleep is the sleep of death. So if you are not dreaming, you know your problem.

WHAT IT IS TO DREAM

To dream in this context has nothing at all to do with sleep. It has everything to do with being wide awake and using the creative power of your brain, using your imagination. To dream, to develop a vision, is to project yourself mentally beyond the crippling confines of your present circumstances into a glorious tomorrow. Dreaming or holding a vision brings the future into being. You can be flat broke, but if you use your brain, you can achieve incredible riches. You are never broke until you give up.

Dreaming strongly and holding on to your dream has the uncanny ability to change your negative circumstances into a positive reality.

THE RETICULAR ACTIVITY SYSTEM (RAS)

Scientists have discovered a section of the brain that they call the RAS. Some people call it the subconscious. It is totally neutral and acts only upon the thoughts that are repeatedly fed into it. It drives you relentlessly to achieve what you believe. This is why the Bible says, "As a man thinketh, so is he". The RAS of your brain will produce in your reality that which you ponder continuously. So powerful is the RAS it has been known to reverse disease.

This story bears repeating:

My friend, Margie, was diagnosed with cancer and given three months to live. She refused to accept this sentence of death and went up into a mountain cottage alone. She walked around speaking out aloud, in every waking moment, "I shall not die, but live! I reject this sentence of death". She changed her diets to nuts and whole foods and transmitted the words of her mouth to her RAS. The cancer went into remission and instead of living for three months, she lived another 20 years! What is more, the last 20 years were her best.

AMBITION

The power of the RAS is seen in what you can achieve by mentally projecting yourself out of your circumstances and into success. When I was a boy, I lived up the road in Old Harbour from another boy. We called him Brookie. Looking at him then, there was nothing that told us that he would achieve anything great. We were just ordinary boys, running around in Old Harbour. But he had a dream, an ambition to serve his country. While the rest of us were playing marbles and eating guineps, he was programming his RAS. Who is he? He is Bruce Golding, who became prime minister of Jamaica.

Hold on to your dreams. Don't let them die. If you believe, the sky is the limit.

Dreamers are achievers.

STRATEGY 2

FROM RAGS TO RICHES:
How the Power of a Dream Affected a Son of St. Ann

Some men see things as they are and say, "Why".
I dream of things that never were and say, "Why not?"
—GEORGE BERNARD SHAW

Years ago a young man came into my insurance office. I had just been appointed branch manager and this rural, rustic young man was seeking a job as a salesman. My first impression of him was completely negative and, I thought to myself, "I will listen to him politely and send him on his way, back to St. Ann." As he entered my office, I could see that he was unkempt and disheveled. His hair was uncombed, his shirt out of his pants, he stuttered so much I thought he was suffering from a speech defect and, clearly, the Queen's English was his distant acquaintance.

I asked him some questions that were designed to relax him. Then I got to the real man. I found out that although not much educated, he was extremely intelligent. By then I had learned that education and intelligence were not necessarily synonymous. I learned that he could not pursue a scholarship to attend Kingston Technical High School because his parents could not afford to relocate him. At that point, he told me, "I realised money was somehow linked to success, and I want to earn money, lots of it."

In those days, there were no psychometric tests for me to employ in assessing his suitability for sales, but I saw something. I saw a fire inside him, a fire of desire which burned so brightly I almost had to put my dark glasses on. I hired him on a hunch, purely on what I construed to be unusual desire, a drive to lift himself from the crippling confines of poverty into financial prosperity.

I taught him how to dress, to speak and to banish his natural diffidence. As he absorbed the training, he became my number one agent. He shattered the New Man record in his first month, producing an astonishing amount of business which, ironically, led me to the first firing of an agent, because an older, non-producing, negative agent had told him, "Don't expect to produce at this level again. We all started this way, but eventually we fall off." I fired him because he was poisoning the limitless mind of this young man. The name of this new recruit was Leopold "Steely" Williams.

TURNING POINT

One morning I took Leopold for breakfast at the then Sheraton Hotel. I had read the book Think and Grow Rich by Napoleon Hill, and I decided to sow a seed in Leopold's mind. I drove him up to Beverley Hills in my Mercedes Benz and we got out next to some of those fantastic houses. I pointed to one particular, fabulously constructed house and said to Leopold: "Steely, one like this can be yours." He gave his usual half smile, looked at me in surprise and said, "Chief, are you serious? Do you really think I could own a house like this?" "Surely," I replied, "for whatever the mind of man can conceive and believe, it can achieve." That quotation from Napoleon Hill was to become the motto of the St. Andrew Circle Branch of Life of Jamaica, a branch I had the honour to lead.

At our next branch retreat, Leopold made an announcement which caused great laughter among his colleagues. We had the habit of meeting every January to set our year's goals, and everyone had to verbalise them. Leopold said, to much laughter, "I have three goals. First, I am going to buy a 'Benz'. Second, I am going to build a big house by the seaside. Third, I am going to retire at 45."

Leopold immediately set to work. He broke all the existing production records at Life of Jamaica and was their leading agent. He bought his Benz, built his house in Discovery Bay by the seaside, as he saw it in his dream. Finally, he retired from LOJ at age 44, one year earlier than he said he would, but not before becoming manager of the Ocho Rios branch.

Today, he is a multi-millionaire, with hundreds of millions of dollars in real estate and more wealth than he would ever admit to. I spoke with him recently and he said, "You know chief (he still calls me chief), it was that vision you gave me on top of Beverley Hills. When I saw your Mercedes parked beside those houses, I said, 'Why not me?' Believe me chief, whatever the mind of man can conceive and believe, it can achieve." So let it be written, so let it be done.

STRATEGY 2

Tapping the Unseen Ability Within

In great attempts it is glorious even to fail.
—VINCE LOMBARDI

The Annual Meeting of the Million Dollar Round Table of life insurance professionals is a forum where great stories are told and where one receives tremendous motivation.

As a youngster in the business, I heard the following story which was indelibly etched upon my mind. It stirred me greatly then, as it does now. Let me share it with you. The "football" referred to is American-style football.

There was a skinny little junior high school boy who loved football. He gave everything he had at practice, but because he was half the size of the other boys, he hardly ever got to play.

Even though the boy sat on the bench, game after game, his father never missed a game. When he entered high school, he was still the smallest of the class but he was determined to go out for football, even though his father told him that he didn't have to play if he didn't want to. All through high school he never missed a practice or a game; but remained a bench warmer. His faithful father was always in the stands, cheering him and encouraging him on.

When he entered college, he decided to try out for the football team as a "walk-on". Everyone was sure he could never make the cut, but he did. The coach admitted that he kept him on the roster because he always seemed to put his heart and soul into every practice, and he pushed the other team members.

He was so excited about making the cut that he rushed to call his father. His father shared his excitement and was sent season tickets for all the college games. During his four years at college, the boy never missed practice; yet he never got to play in a game.

At the end of his senior football season, as he ran onto the practice field shortly before the big playoff game, the coach met him with a telegram. He read it, swallowed hard, then mumbled to the coach: "My father died this morning. Is it alright if I miss practice today?" The coach put his arm around his shoulder and said, "Take the rest of the week off, son. And don't even plan to come back to the game on Saturday."

Saturday arrived, and the game was not going well. In the third quarter, with the team ten points behind, the young man quietly slipped into the empty locker room and pulled on his football gear. As he ran onto the sidelines, the coach and players were stunned to see him back so soon.

He approached the coach and begged him to let him play but the coach pretended not to hear him, as he was not going to put his worst player in this close playoff game. But the young man continued to beg him, and finally, feeling sorry for him, the coach gave in.

Before long, the coach, the players, and everyone in the stands could not believe their eyes. This guy, who had never played before, was doing everything right. He ran, passed, blocked and tackled brilliantly. The score was soon tied. In the closing seconds of the game, he intercepted a pass and ran all the way for the winning touchdown. His teammates hoisted him onto their shoulders as the fans erupted.

After the stands had emptied and the team had left the locker room, the coach noticed that his young hero was sitting in the corner all alone. The coach approached him and said, "Kid, I can't believe it. You were fantastic! Tell me, what got into you? How did you do it?"

He looked at the coach, tears in his eyes, and said, "Well, you knew my dad died, but did you know that my dad was blind?"

He forced a smile. "Dad came to all of my games, but today was the first time he could see me play, and I wanted to show him I could do it!"

STRATEGY 2

People Who Succeeded Against the Odds

It doesn't matter if you come from the inner city.
People who fail in life are people who find lots of excuses.
It's never too late for a person to recognise that they
have potential in themselves. —BENJAMIN CARSON

History is full of stories of people who succeeded against staggering odds; people who were told their situation was hopeless. But they refused to let other people define what they could or could not do. Les Brown, the renowned international motivational speaker was told that he was "academically retarded" and when a teacher asked him to write something on a board, he refused, telling the teacher that he had been described as "academically retarded." The teacher looked him squarely in the eye and told him, "Young man, never, never, NEVER, accept someone else's definition of your capabilities. Let NO ONE tell you what you cannot do!" Brown said that changed his life and today an "academically retarded" man is a multi-millionaire and a great motivational speaker.

The famous brain surgeon, Dr. Ben Carson, was told he was a dunce and could not make it academically. But his mother told him he could achieve anything he wanted, if he only believed in himself. It worked. Today he is world famous—a former "dunce!"

After a lifetime of defeats, at 62, Winston Churchill became one of Britain's greatest prime ministers. And Abraham Lincoln racked up a string of defeats before he became president of the United States. And what obstacles did Barack Obama have to overcome to be where he is today?

You too can succeed against the odds, for deep within you lies awesome power, the power to turn dreams into reality and to achieve greatness in life. All you need is a vision of greatness, a written down plan and a commitment to work as if everything depends on it.

STRATEGY 2

Living Above Your Circumstances

If you will call your troubles experiences, and remember that every experience develops some latent force within you, you will grow vigorous and happy, however adverse your circumstances may seem to be. —JOHN R. MILLER

Years ago when Jamaica was in great political and economic upheaval, I met a friend from England. He asked me how I was doing. I replied, "Harry, under the circumstances, I am not doing too badly." Quickly he replied, "Tony, what in heaven's name are you doing UNDER the circumstances? You should be above them!" As I reflected upon what he said to me, it dawned on me, that it's your attitude towards life that determines life's attitude towards you. You may not be able to control the wind, but you can set your sail.

The great cop-out in life, the most frequent excuse for failure and non-achievement is "circumstance." Circumstances are the happenstance of life. It is a waste of time to moan and groan about your circumstances.

You can change your circumstances by changing your attitude, by living above them, by harnessing the powers of your God-given brain, by developing a vision. Vision is the starting point of success. The absence of it is a death sentence, for without a vision, people perish.

STRATEGY 2

Living the Dream... From Hospital Bed to Hospital Boss

Never Give in! Never! Never!! Never!!!
—SIR WINSTON CHURCHILL

There is often a long, hard, treacherous road between the dream and the reality. Having the dream is one thing; fulfilling the dream is quite another story. It takes determination, fighting obstacles, falling and rising again.

Madline Audrey Hinchcliffe is one Jamaican superstar living her dream. In fact, her story epitomises what it takes to fulfill a dream. She was boarded out as a child, and described the experience as "hell". She was mistreated. But she had a dream instilled in her young subconscious by her father who told her, "You must make something of yourself". In 1958 she entered nursing school at UHWI and for most of the time was sick with nephritis. She spent an additional six months catching up with her studies and recovering from another illness, tonsillitis with complications that arose from a tonsillectomy. She almost did not graduate; but she did, for she had a dream.

She graduated in 1961 and started working in Mandeville in August 1962. While doing the job of nursing, she ended up on the hospital bed with a ruptured appendix—a life threatening condition. There were complications—she could not wake up from the anesthesia—they fought and saved her life.

Later married, she became very ill with both her pregnancies, and almost died of kidney disease and hemorrhaging in childbirth. To top it all, her marriage dissolved. The father of her children then died suddenly. Virtually penniless and left with two children to support, she migrated to the USA. She worked three jobs simultaneously, furthered her education, and sent her children to school.

She studied hard, ended up on the dean's list and graduated. She told me, "Tony, at my graduation, I heard only two little hands clapping in the audience—my two children saying, "Go, Mom!"

As she studied, her dream began to grow. "Why be a nurse?" she asked herself. "Why not run the hospital? After all, this is where the big money is."

No sooner than she received this bigger dream, she was hit again with sickness, and septicemia after surgery almost took her life. She spent six weeks in a hospital bed. But she held on to her new dream and was appointed director of nursing and also became a college professor. She moved to the University Hospital of Jacksonville, Florida and turned it around administratively.

In 1980, she fell ill again—another six weeks in hospital. Friends had to assist her financially and look after her children. She subsequently lost the position in Jacksonville, but in 1982 was recruited by the CARICOM Secretariat in Guyana as health development officer for the region. She took ill with a heart condition and ended up in the ICU at the Princess Margaret hospital in Barbados. On a trip to India she lost most of her hair with a botched hairdo in which the chemicals used on her hair were so powerful no hair would re-grow. She has sported the bald look ever since.

In May 1987 she came home. "I always wanted to come back to Jamaica", she said. She came home, but no one would hire her. Rejection after rejection! She sought counseling for she thought now of going back to America. She was given this advice by the counselor: "There are several Jamaicas and you must choose which Jamaica you want to live in." She owed over five months' rent for her little office, three months' arrears on her mortgage, her phone was cut off. Yet she had a dream. She was determined to succeed.

She started Caribbean Health Consultants Limited, and got little or no work as competition came out of the woodwork. Broke and disappointed, she started to close her office in preparation to remigrate, when a letter came from Maxine Henry Wilson offering her a consultancy at the Social Development Commission (SDC). She sat down and wept. This was the break she needed! Through this one contract from the SDC, Caribbean Health Consultants Limited had a rebirth.

She started to tender for hospital services, and in 1990 won the tender for the Tony Thwaites wing at the UHWI. In 1993 she won a tender to provide janitorial services for the Spanish Town Hospital. She started out with eighteen workers at the Tony Thwaites wing and as they say, the rest is history. Today, Audrey Hinchcliffe lives her dream in Manpower and Maintenance Services Limited, employing up to 2000 workers. Her accolades and awards are numerous and earned her the names "phenomenal woman", "queen of clean".

I asked her what advice she would give, now that she is eminently successful. She said, "Don't let discouragement get you down. Go in for the long haul; know when to seek help. Measure success in small units. Never give up. What you think is failure tonight could be success tomorrow morning". If Audrey Hinchcliffe can live her dream, so can you!

STRATEGY 2

How Dreaming Becomes a Creative Vision

*We grow by dreams. All big men are dreamers.
Some of us let our dreams die but others nourish and protect them,
nurse them through bad days…to the sunshine and light
which always come.* —WOODROW WILSON

I dream of Life of Jamaica as a household name.
—R. DANNY WILLIAMS,

Many years ago, as a young life insurance salesman, I was given a book by my friend and Calabar schoolmate, Arnold "Scree" Bertram. That book was to change the course of my life. It was *Think and Grow Rich*, by Napoleon Hill. Scree, young and idealistic in the tumultuous events of the radical '60s said, as he gave me the book: "Tony, this book is about wealth creation. That is not what I am seeking, but its principles are amazing. I am going to use these principles to change Jamaica politically. Scree, along with a group of young thinkers, went on to help Michael Manley make important changes to the social fabric of our country. One touching example was Manley's abolition of the illegitimacy law or "law of bastardy" where children born out of wedlock could not inherit property. Manley and this group also improved the status of women with a far more liberal allocation of maternity leave with pay, allowing nursing mothers to spend time with their infants.

Not long after reading Think and Grow Rich, I heard a speech that greatly impacted my thinking. The speaker made the point that a dream strongly held produced the thing desired. He said thoughts are things, and thoughts will produce the things we constantly think about, good or evil. He gave several examples of people who, desiring what seemed like the impossible, achieved the impossible. One of these was Henry Ford who was told by his engineers that the development of the V-8 engine was an engineering impossibility. Ford's reply was, "I can see it in my mind. If I can see it, it must be possible. Go back to the drawing board." After several attempts, they did the impossible, and the V-8 engine is now ancient history.

As a Christian, I decided to check the Bible to see if this principle of a creative vision was there. I found it all over the New Testament! I also found it in the life of Job, the man who became sick and lost all of his wealth. To my amazement, I found that Job's thinking became a negative creative vision, bringing into reality what he was thinking about. Job says:

"For the thing which I greatly feared is come upon me, and that which I was afraid of is come unto me". (Job 3:25)

From his own confession, Job's thought process attracted into his life the very thing he "greatly feared."

When I reviewed the lives of Marcus Garvey, Mahatma Ghandi, Billy Graham, Ken Hall, Audrey Hinchcliffe, Nelson Mandela, Michael Manley, Merlene Ottey, Edward Seaga, Garfield Sobers, Danny Williams, and many other high achievers, I concluded that their driving force was a whip called desire, a mighty force called a dream.

A dream leads to desire, and intense desire is creative, for good or ill. Hitler had a dream, a "creative" vision that unleashed overwhelming destruction upon Europe. Marcus Garvey had a dream, a creative vision that inspired thousands of black people across the diaspora to be proud of their race that lifted people of African origins to "Up you mighty race".

Any dream, any desire strongly held, leads to the achievement, for good or ill, of the dream held. This then, is a creative vision. It starts with a dream, it becomes a desire, it then grows into an overwhelming passion, a magnificent obsession or malevolent madness… then it becomes reality.

SPEECH AND REPETITION

Your mind will express itself in your speech. What your speech constantly repeats is transmitted to your subconscious. Your subconscious is like a blotter; it soaks up the ink of thought and words. It is neutral, it does not know fear or failure, success or achievement. It is programmed by your thought life, by your speech, by your dreams, by your desire. Think positively, your life is programmed that way. Think negatively, you will have the biblical Job experience. Your programmed subconscious moves you relentlessly, inexorably, to achieve what you dream.

Dream big dreams for, as Stephen Locke puts it, "It may be that those who do most, dream most".

Strategy 3
CREATE A FOOLPROOF PLAN TO SUCCEED

STRATEGY 3

GOAL SETTING: Master Key to Turning Visions into Reality

A man without a goal is like a ship without a rudder.
—THOMAS CARLYSLE

I have been writing about the tremendous power of the mind, the need to dream and then to move that dream to desire, intense desire. This desire grows so great, it becomes a creative vision. But a vision is useless unless it is transformed into reality. There is a process by which you can turn your dreams into reality, and it starts with planning. It continues with work, very hard work of which you will learn later on in this book.

Goals are the signposts of life. Someone said, "If you don't know where you are going, any road will take you there." If you do not have a goal, you do not have purpose. Remember this "P"-ditty:

No Purpose, no Pursuit;
No Pursuit, no Passion;

No Passion, no Power;
No Power, no Prize.

Without a goal, you drift aimlessly like flotsam and jetsam (ocean debris) in life's turbulent seas, like dead fish carried downstream by the river of life. If you aim at nothing, you hit nothing. It will be well worth your while to memorise the words of American naturalist Henry David Thoreau:

"In the long run, men hit only at what they aim. Therefore, though they should fail immediately, it is best they aim at something high."

John F. Kennedy puts it this way; "Effort and courage are not enough without purpose and direction". Where are you aiming? What goals do you have? What is your purpose in life?

Let us then begin to turn our visions into reality by setting some goals. Here are four steps:

1. SET CLEARLY DEFINED GOALS AND WRITE THEM DOWN

In the 1950s, a study was made of the graduating class of a large university in America. The researchers followed their progress for twenty years and at the end of that time, they made the following discovery:

Three percent of the class had written out, clearly defined goals. Ninety-seven percent had not written down any goals. The three percent of graduates with written down goals had not only surpassed their goals, but their incomes were three times larger than the 97 percent who had not written down clearly defined goals! The researchers concluded that goals, when clearly defined and written down, are usually achieved.

2. BREAK DOWN LARGE GOALS INTO SMALLER PORTIONS

The life insurance industry recognises Ben Feldman as the greatest salesman of the 20th century. In 1970, Feldman alone produced

US$100 million dollars in business—more business than many life companies. Ben was asked how he could conceive of, much less produce such an astronomical sum of business. He replied, "Well, if you look at it as $100 million, it's big. But if you break it down to $2 million per week, it's really no big thing." The secret of eating an elephant is "one bite at a time."

If you work, say on commissions, break down your goals to the daily earnings that you require.

3. SET SPECIFIC TIME PERIODS FOR THE ACCOMPLISHMENT OF YOUR GOALS

The advantage of specific times that will signal the accomplishment of your goals is the focus that it creates. Time constraints focus the mind. In fact, there is a saying (referring to a condemned man) that "there is nothing that concentrates the mind more than a hanging next morning." Set short term, medium term and long term goals, and evaluate your progress as you go along.

4. SHARE "GIVE UP" GOALS WITH MANY, "GO UP" GOALS WITH ONLY A FEW

Give up goals fall in the category of giving up something for your betterment. For example, you may share your goal to give up smoking on the 1st of January. Or, you may share your goal to lose 25lbs by March 31. People will support you in these "give up" goals.

Be careful, however, how you share your "go up" goals. Let me give you an example. Suppose you desire to become the president or managing director of your company; if you share that with people who have the same ambition, you are not likely to receive their support since you are competing against them. You may only succeed in creating tension at the workplace, so be very selective with whom you share "go up" goals. If you set goals, plan your work and work your plan, your visions will be turned into reality.

STRATEGY 3

Making the Most of Priorities

*The passing moment is all we can be sure of;
it is only common sense to extract its utmost
value from it.* —W. SOMERSET MAUGHAM

In the 1920's Charles Schwab, president of Bethlehem Steel Company in the United States, posed an unusual challenge to Ivy Lee, an efficiency consultant. "Show me a way to get more things done with my time," Schwab said, "and I'll pay you any fee within reason."

"Fine", answered Lee. "I can give you something in twenty minutes that will improve your results from action and doing by at least 50 percent."

"Okay", Schwab said, "let's have it now, for twenty minutes is just about all the time I have before my train leaves."

Lee took out a blank sheet of paper from his pocket and handed it to Schwab.

"Write on this piece of paper the six most important tasks you have to do tomorrow". Schwab took three minutes to write down the tasks.

"Now", Lee continued, "number them in order of their importance", Schwab did that in five minutes. "Now", said Lee, "put this paper in your pocket and tomorrow morning, first thing, look at item one and start working on it until it is finished. Go to item two and tackle that the same way; then item three, and so on. Do this until your day ends. Do not be concerned if you have only finished one or two. You'll be working on the most important ones. If you can't finish them all by this method, you couldn't have done so with any other method either, and without some system, you'd probably not even have decided which item was the most important."

Lee finished by saying to Schwab, "Do this every working day. If you feel it works for you, have your employees try it for themselves. Try it for as long as you wish, and if it works send me a cheque for what you think it is worth." This whole interview took less than twenty minutes and Schwab departed.

After a few weeks Schwab sent Lee a cheque for $25,000 with a letter saying that this piece of advice generated him more profits than from any other single piece of advice he had ever received. In five years this plan turned Bethlehem Steel Company into the largest producer of steel in the world and helped to put one hundred million dollars in the pocket of Charles Schwab.

I came upon this story in August, 1969 from a book loaned to me by a young playwright named Trevor Rhone. I had been recently married and was contemplating entering the life insurance industry. Trevor lived in the same apartment complex and we struck up a relationship. He was writing a play about life insurance salesmen, and when I shared with him my interest and my wife's concerns, he loaned me some of his research material. I took this one idea called a "To Do" list and I have worked with it since then. People often are curious about how I organise myself but the idea came from the "To Do" list and Charles Schwab.

WHY YOU SHOULD USE A TO DO LIST

Time is precious, and whether you are the managing director of a large corporation, a salesman, a housewife, a pastor, or a social worker, you can have no finer organiser of your time than a daily "To Do" list. If you work with a personal pocket computer or organiser, it's the section called "Tasks."

At the end of your day, set aside fifteen minutes to write down (or type in) tomorrow's tasks. Record them as they come to mind. After you have written out the tasks, go back over your list and number them in order of priority or importance:

#1 being the most important

#2 the next most important, and so on

Start your day by tackling number one, exactly as Charles Schwab did. When you accomplish it, cross out the entry with a straight line. Whatever you have not crossed out was not accomplished. You simply carry these over to the next day's "To Do" list, and repeat every working day.

You will find, as I have done over the last forty-five years that this one act is the single most important tool of time and self-management every day. Try it; it works.

STRATEGY 3

ACHIEVING SUCCESS WITH A D.O.M.E. PLAN: Diagnosis

Things may come to those who wait, but only the things left by those who hustle. —ABRAHAM LINCOLN

Some decades ago, the Life Insurance Marketing & Research Association (LIMRA) recommended a formula for success in one's chosen career. Over the years, thousands of persons inside and outside of the life insurance profession have used this formula to achieve success, not only in their careers, but also in life as a whole. The formula is described in an acronym called DOME:

Diagnosis

Objectives

Methods

Evaluation

These four areas of engagement, if properly understood and appropriated, can propel you to success in your career, your family life, your spiritual life, your health, your finances or just about any area you choose at whatever age you are. In this article, we shall use career goals to explain the DOME. I will only analyse Diagnosis in this section. I shall consider Objectives, Methods and Evaluation later on in the book.

DIAGNOSIS

In order to properly start the process of the realisation of your goals and dreams, it is necessary to ask yourself, "What is my situation now?" This is called diagnosis. Doctors know that proper diagnosis is indispensable to successful treatment. Similarly, you must know where you are in order to better know where you ought to go, and how you are going to get there.

Many persons have never taken an inventory of where they are on the road of life. When they do, many realise that they are nowhere near where they want to be, as time rushes by leaving them staring blankly into the future like a cow at a new gate.

So what about you? Are you where you want to be in life?

Have you analysed your present situation? If not, let's do so now.

Get a sheet of paper and write down the answers to these questions that you must now ask yourself:

- Am I where I plan to be in my career?
- Am I satisfied with my progress?
- Have I done the appropriate studies?
- Am I satisfied with my income?
- Where do I plan to be in five years' time?
- For your family life, you could ask questions like these:
- Am I spending time with my children?
- Is my love-life fulfilling?
- Am I carrying resentment towards my spouse?
- Are we, as a family realising our goals—financial, spiritual, health?

SWOT ANALYSIS

SWOT is an acronym for strengths, weaknesses, opportunities and threats. To assist you in the diagnosis, do a personal SWOT analysis and write your findings down on paper:

What are my <u>strengths</u>?

What are my <u>weaknesses</u>?

What <u>opportunities</u> lie before me?

Are there any <u>threats</u> to the success of my career?

Be brutally frank with your answers. When you identify weaknesses or threats, write out a plan to deal with these. Get professional advice if you need it.

Here is something important to know: Most successful people do not spend their time trying to improve their weaknesses. They concentrate on maximising their strengths. They find a way to cope with their weaknesses, but they work assiduously on their strengths. If you find physics or mathematics difficult, there's little point studying to be a rocket scientist. You may, however, have tremendous persuasion skills that might make you an excellent lawyer.

As far as strengths are concerned, write these out as they come to mind. Then go back over the strengths and prioritise them, #1 being the strongest, #2 the next strongest, and so on. Now attach to each a plan to make your strengths even better, or to utilise them more. For example, if one of your strengths is leadership, secure some books on leadership and read them. Then offer yourself in leadership—to mentor someone, to teach a class, to lead a weekend trip to Cuba.

Of which opportunities can your strengths take advantage? Do you have a good command of spoken English? Is your voice pleasant? Then look at radio or television that might maximise these strengths and multiply your income.

And what threats would hinder you? Identify them first, then plan to go around them, over them or tunnel under them. Where there is a will there's a way.

Where your weaknesses are concerned, make a note of them but do not be overly preoccupied with them unless such weaknesses involve anti-social behavior or character flaws. In these cases, seek professional help and counseling. But, if you are not very good at skydiving, perhaps baking or floral arranging is where your talent is. You can certainly make additional income from baking and selling cakes.

When this diagnosis is complete, you must have a written document setting out strengths, weaknesses, opportunities and threats. Only then are you ready for the next three stages of the D.O.M.E. Plan.

STRATEGY 3

ACHIEVING SUCCESS WITH A **D.O.M.E.** PLAN: Objectives

Luck is what happens when preparation meets opportunity.
—ELMER LETTERMAN

You previously read about DIAGNOSIS as the first part of the D.O.M.E. Plan—a highly successful planning tool for achieving success in life. The acronym DOME stands for diagnosis, objectives, methods, evaluation. In this section, I share with you some thoughts on setting your objectives in life, and fixing your goals for success.

OBJECTIVES

Successful people the world over are goal oriented. Yogi Berra, in his own inimitable style, puts it this way: "If you don't know where you are going in life, you're liable to wind up somewhere else". If you put Yogi's statement another way, it really asks, "If you don't know where you are going, how will you ever know when you get there?"

In 1865, the famous writer Lewis Carroll wrote a magnificent children's classic, Alice's Adventures in Wonderland. In the story, Alice chases a rabbit down a rabbit hole and meets all kinds of strange creatures in this weird, topsy-turvy world. On her journey, she meets the grinning Cheshire Cat reposing on a branch in a tree beside the road. Here now, is the dialogue between the two, a dialogue which speaks so profoundly to the lack of a specific goal:

> "Would you tell me, please, which way I ought to go from here?'
>
> "That depends a good deal on where you want to get to," said the Cat.
>
> "I don't much care where," said Alice.
>
> "Then it doesn't matter which way you go," said the Cat.
>
> "…so long as I get somewhere," Alice added as an explanation.
>
> "Oh, you're sure to do that," said the Cat.

If you have no goals, you achieve little. If you aim at nothing, you hit nothing.

BE, DO, HAVE

There are three little verbs that should guide your goals—be, do, have. What do you want to be? What do you want to do? What do you want to have? "Be" speaks to character development, integrity and inner strength. This must be first on your goals, for if you have wealth and no character you are a potential walking disaster.

TIME HORIZONS

Set goals and include a time horizon for their achievement. Be specific where possible, for goals must be measurable. Do not set as a goal, "I plan to be rich". Instead, state the amount of money you intend to have in the bank, by when it will be there and how you intend to acquire it (methods). Write these down. It is virtually useless to say, "I must buy my own house". Instead, write out the plan, including the time when you will do the purchase, where the house will be, what it will cost, what the house will look like.

It does not matter whether you have the funds at the present time. What is important is for you to envision the house, believe it will become a reality and work like a dog for its achievement.

LIFETIME GOALS

A DOME plan works not only for your career but in every other area of your life. What do you want to achieve for the rest of your life? How would you like to spend the next three years? Alan Lakein suggests that we all ask ourselves this most important question: "If you knew you would be struck dead by lightning six months from today, how would you live until then?" Commit your thoughts to paper.

Think carefully about this question. If you knew you would be struck dead by lightning six months from today, you would probably squeeze into that limited time whatever you consider important. Now, do this exercise, without including plans for your funeral. Get a piece of paper and quickly write out what you would do and how you would spend your last six months. Do this in no more than three minutes. When you make this list, it will show you what is <u>really</u> important to you that you are probably not doing now. The activities on this list deserve more of your attention for the next six months.

After you have done this written exercise, there are two other written exercises you should undertake. Write out how you would like to live your life for the next three years. Then finally, write out your lifetime goals. Quickly write out the things that come to mind—do not take more than three minutes to do each section. Then go back over each list (six months, three years, lifetime) and prioritise each goal with an ABC system. 'A' goals are the most important to you. 'B' goals are the next most important ones, and 'C' goals come next. The ABC priority system helps you to resolve competing goals. If you set a high priority on going back to school, then you may feel that family time for instance ranks below that. This conflict might be resolved by making both of these 'A' goals. You could further refine your top three goals by describing them A1, A2, A3.

STRATEGY 3

ACHIEVING SUCCESS WITH A D.O.M.E. PLAN: Methods

We're like bicycles, which stand upright as long as we have forward motion towards a goal. But we, like bicycles, fall when we no longer have direction in our lives.
—LEWIS TIMBERLAKE

We are dealing with the acronym DOME—diagnosis, objectives, methods, evaluation. DOME is a proven formula for success. In this section we continue our thoughts on <u>methods</u> (work). We will not achieve our goals by wishing and dreaming. Goals will only be achieved by intelligent, self-directed goals, driven by "blood, sweat and tears". Successful people work hard, very hard, ten—sixteen hours per day towards specific objectives. An eight-hour work day, especially for a person just starting professional life, is only flattering to deceive. If you work for a salary or fixed wages for eight hours per day, you are treading water.

LIFE'S COMPENSATIONS

When I got married in 1968, I placed a plaque over the section of the kitchen where I knew my wife would see it. It was intended to be funny, but it carried an element of humorous truth. It said (to my wife):

"How to act like a lady

How to look like a girl and…

How to WORK LIKE A DOG!"

An affable, even-tempered, unruffled lady, she never moved that plaque and I kept seeing, "How to work like a dog", every time I opened the refrigerator (which I did frequently). That repetition entered my subconscious and it was I who ended up working like a dog! Now here is a beautiful compensation about life. Where work is concerned, this is true:

"DO MORE THAN YOU ARE PAID FOR,

AND YOU WILL BE

PAID FOR MORE THAN YOU DO."

An inviolable law is this: Whatever you sow in work, you reap in success. For thirty-eight years, I have had the pleasure of working with, training and developing life insurance agents. I have always made the point to them that no great achievement is ever made without hard, indefatigable, persistent work. Most agents fail not because of ability, but because of laziness, lack of focus, lack of planning, believing that four hours a day will make them super salespeople. Many fell into the trap of pushing paper in the office, running quotations, not realizing that seeing the people was the key to their success. But those who went beyond the boundaries of mediocrity in their work became successful.

THAT EXTRA EFFORT

Life is no man's debtor. Life pays you exactly what you bargain for. If you bargain with life for a penny, life will pay you no more. Young people make one huge mistake; they first concern themselves with high income. So many people come to me seeking help, and they start with, "My salary is so small. I need another job." But this is putting the cart before the horse, balancing the triangle on its apex rather than on its base. My response to them is usually this, "Fine. But what will you exchange for this high income?"

People will not simply pay you a high income because you think you deserve it, or have several degrees at the end of your name. Degrees do not do the work. It is you who must do the work. It's not the MBA that's important. It's what services, goods or products are you prepared to exchange for your income. Young people ought not to first be preoccupied with a high income. They should be preoccupied with hard work, long hours, gaining experience, thrifty living and great goals. In their early years, income might be small but as they put in the hard work, income comes in torrents as they make a name for themselves later in life.

Get into the habit of making that extra effort, of rising early, studying your line of business, working hard and expecting greatness. If you are in sales, remember the three rules of success, "See the people. See the people. See the people." In the beginning, we make our habits, in the end our habits make us. Do not expect to walk into your job at the top, for there are very few occupations where you start at the top. One of them is grave digging.

Above all, whatever you do, do more than you are paid for, for eventually life will pay you more than you do.

STRATEGY 3

ACHIEVING SUCCESS WITH A **D.O.M.E.** PLAN: Evaluation

I find it much more sensible to pause and sharpen my axe than to continue chopping the tree with a dull axe.
—CLARENCE DENNY

I receive considerable amounts of email from persons responding to my weekly newspaper column, *Dollar for Your Thoughts*. When I analyse many of these responses, I find that the failure to achieve is not in the absence of dreams, but in the failure to manage the methods, or, said another way, the stabbing in the dark at a moving target. You can turn around your life by regularly taking time out to examine your progress, finding out where you are, and correcting any problems while they are still small ones. It is an easy thing to lose three pounds, but quite another matter to lose 30. But when did the three pounds become 30 lbs? While we were eating and not evaluating our weight!

It was Albert Einstein who said, "Insanity is doing the same thing and expecting different results." Perhaps regular evaluation of your progress is where you need to do things differently. Many people ask me about diabetes management, and when I ask them "what is their average blood glucose reading over the last three months", they don't have a clue. But successful management of diabetes, like successful management of your goals, involves constant evaluation, including your daily blood sugar testing.

Former group managing director of NCB, Aubyn Hill, a highly successful man, says, "Eighty percent of good management is follow-up." An evaluation, check or follow-up on your progress is a necessary part of your success. If you are blown off course, the sooner you know and correct it, the better.

A LESSON FROM AN AIR JAMAICA FLIGHT

Some years ago, I flew with my pilot friend in the cockpit jump seat of an Air Jamaica jetliner. I watched the dials as he took the plane seven miles high and powered the massive jet at 600 miles per hour across the Atlantic. According to the instrument panel readings which were being evaluated minute-by-minute, we were encountering jet stream winds at over 100 miles per hour, blowing diagonally across the plane. The flight path had to be corrected time and again to keep it on course and to land us precisely at the agreed location. At the point where we were then, an uncorrected deviation of one degree takes the airplane 60 miles off target. My friend said to me, "Tony, a successful flight is really a series of midcourse corrections." And it struck me: a successful life (or career) is like a successful flight; it's a series of midcourse corrections. You may be blown off course by many things—sickness, disappointments, migration, economics or whatever. Evaluation makes you aware of your "flight path" and allows you to correct it so you land precisely at your destination.

Failure to evaluate your progress as you pursue your goals is one reason so many people never achieve their New Year's resolutions. They decide to lose 25lb and wonder why twelve months later they have gained weight rather than lost weight. They did not evaluate their progress. Many were afraid of what the scale would tell them.

Success can be defined in many ways, but I have always liked Albert Grey's definition of success. He said, "The common denominator of all success lies in forming the habit of doing things that failures don't like to do." Failures do not evaluate their progress on any regular basis. You cannot run a business without timely knowledge and evaluation of your income and expenditure. Joseph Matalon once said to me, "Management gets what it inspects, not what it expects." Evaluation is about management, and if you cannot manage yourself, you are not likely to be able to manage others.

Develop your DOME plan—**Diagnosis, Objectives, Methods and Evaluation**. It is worth your investment in time and effort, and could make the difference between average performance and spectacular achievement. Choosing to do the DOME would be one of your most important choices for your career because, "Destiny is not a matter of chance; it is a matter of choice."

STRATEGY 3

How a D.O.M.E. Plan Saved a Life

It must be borne in mind that the tragedy of life doesn't lie in not reaching your goal. The tragedy lies in having no goal to reach. It isn't calamity to die with dreams unfulfilled, but it is a calamity not to dream. It is not a disaster to be unable to capture your ideal, but it is a disaster to have no ideal to capture. It is not a disgrace not to reach the stars, but it is a disgrace to have no stars to reach for. Not failure, but low aim is sin. —DR. BENJAMIN E. MAYS
SCHOLAR, EDUCATOR, AND PRESIDENT
EMERITUS OF MOREHOUSE COLLEGE

I have outlined the highly successful planning method embodied in the acronym DOME—diagnosis, objectives, methods and evaluation. For a DOME plan to fix itself into your subconscious mind, it has to be written down on paper. If you do not write it out, you may miss the incredible power of the subconscious objectives that you constantly read and re-read.

What I am going to share with you is a true story. You may find it difficult to believe, but it proves the power of the DOME at any age in life. It also demonstrates that failure is not final.

Failure dominated a certain man's life, misfortune was his twin brother. His father died when he was only five years old and he quit school at sixteen. He married at eighteen, became a father at nineteen and the couple had a wonderful baby daughter; a child he loved with a passion. But at twenty his wife left him and took their baby daughter with her, devastating him. After he married at eighteen, he worked as a railroad conductor and failed at that. He joined the army and crashed out there, farmed some land and made a mess of that too, became a life insurance salesman and failed miserably at that as well. The only thing he could do was to cook, so he became a cook and dishwasher in a small café.

He worked long hard hours in that small, smelly, hot café. As he worked he grieved for his wife and baby daughter. Time after time he begged her to return to him. Time after time she refused. He went down on his knees, he cried, he implored her, but the lady was adamant, she would never return.

So this young, broken-hearted father grew desperate. He loved his daughter with a passion and formulated a plan to get her back. He planned it carefully, mapped out every move. For a week this grief-stricken man hid in the bushes outside his wife's modest home, watching his daughter and planning his next move.

He would kidnap her.

He had worked out the plan to the detail, the timing, and the logistics. The thought that he was about to commit a crime never entered his mind.

The day came when he was to execute this fail-safe plan. Driven by the desperate desire to have his daughter back with him, he positioned himself in the bushes and waited for his daughter to come out and play. He waited, and waited, but that day, his daughter never came out to play. He even failed at committing a crime! At that time he felt himself the ultimate loser, destined to fail at every single thing in life, condemned to spend the rest of his life alone and abandoned.

With time, however, his wife relented and came back to him and together, they worked in the café, working and washing dishes until he retired at sixty-five. On his first day of retirement, the mailman delivered a United States government letter. When he opened it, it was his first Social Security cheque for US$105.00. He looked at the cheque and judged in his mind that the government was now telling him he could no longer take care of himself for the rest of his life. That did it. This cheque summed up for him his entire life of rejection, failure, defeat, demoralisation, wretchedness and serial disappointments. For forty-nine long years he had worked and it had now come down to a Social Security cheque of $105. He reasoned, "If I cannot take care of myself and must now depend upon the government to take care of me, life is not worth living anymore". So he decided to take his own life.

He took up a sheet of paper and a pencil, went outside of his house and sat under a tree. He was about to write his last will and testament. Unknowingly, however, he began to write a DOME plan. He started to write and as he penciled his thoughts he wrote down what his life could have been (Diagnosis); what he should be, what he had planned for the rest of his life (Objectives). There was something he could do that he himself knew he could do better than anyone else knew he could do. He could cook (Methods). In writing out these things a light bulb went off in his head." I'm not finished yet!" he said.

He got up from under the tree, walked into town and went to the bank. He borrowed $87 against his next Social Security cheque. With that $87, he bought some boxes and chicken. He went home and fried the chicken with a special recipe which he had developed while working over the years in that little café. He started to sell the chicken, door to door, in his hometown of Corbin, Kentucky. His name? Colonel Harlan Sanders, the originator of Kentucky Fried Chicken.

As Col. Sanders finished speaking in California, the eighty-eight year old man walked slowly down the steps of the platform assisted by a silver cane. He had finished answering questions to six thousand realtors at a convention. A voice rang out, "Colonel Sanders, how much money are you worth?"

"I don't know, son", he replied, "but if I want it, I can buy it."

At sixty-five he was a monumental failure. At eighty-five, a multi-millionaire, king of the vast KFC empire. Write your DOME plan, work hard and never give up.

Strategy ④
WORK YOUR PLAN, REACH YOUR HIGHEST POTENTIAL

STRATEGY 4

WORK:
The Difference between the Wishbone and the Backbone

As I approached fifty years in the workplace, I can report some very clear experiences and discoveries. I have hired scores of persons, worked with hundreds, seen people rise and fall, observed some spectacular successes and equally spectacular failures. I have worked with prime ministers and paupers. Five percent of people have marched to the top of their fields as leaders. Perhaps another three percent have achieved success, if you define success as the progressive realization of one's own goals. But the vast majority of the working population simply marches to the rhythmic drumbeat of the status quo. Those who place themselves at the bottom of the pile have one mindless phrase they constantly repeat, a demeaning self-fulfilling prophecy, *Nutten na gwan fi mi*. People who repeat this unthinking nonsense are twice dead—dead in ignorance, dead to hope. For, nothing "goes on" for anyone. You have to make it happen. As the saying goes, "If it's going to be, it's up to me."

If you ask me, "what is the most important factor of success in this life?" I would unhesitatingly say "work." Not just brute force, energy expending work, but work to a plan, work towards a goal, thought-inspired work, and work beyond the "average" workday.

Dreaming and envisioning the future are only the starting points of success. But they will be merely daydreams, only the wishbone, if such dreaming is not followed up with work. The dreams of so many people are just that, dreams, and these persons wake up to find themselves at age 65 wondering how much the National Insurance Scheme will provide them upon retirement!

In business, as indicated in previous chapters, the acronym DOME stands for Diagnosis, Objectives, Methods and Evaluation. "Methods" speak to the instruments, the work, the study, and the investment in time, the daily, monthly and yearly "blood, sweat and tears" you put into accomplishing your objectives. There is no free lunch. Vince Lombardi puts it this way: "The only place success comes before work is in the dictionary." Without work, many a beautiful plan evaporates like morning mist under the hot sun. When it comes to work, it is not wishbone—it's backbone.

A BIG MISTAKE IN LIFE—THE EIGHT-HOUR WORK DAY

A high-profile politician spoke with me once, commenting on my series of Dollar For Your Thoughts articles. He said, "Tony, I have no problem with what you are writing, especially when you write stories like the success of Leopold Williams. However, I am seeing more and more of this 'get rich quick mentality', this feeling that 'I must have it all now, at all costs.' People don't seem to make a connection between work and wealth, so they turn to criminal activities to achieve wealth." And of course he is right. I promised him I would write about the importance of work and the link between dreaming and working.

A colossal mistake in life is to believe, especially in your early career, that an eight-hour workday is what you should aim for. Take it from me; an eight-hour workday is a prescription for marginalization, especially if what you receive from it is a salary or some kind of fixed wages. When you work for the first eight hours, you work for other people—the boss, the taxman, the rent man, the utilities company and the credit card company. The next eight hours, you work for yourself. You are not likely to achieve your financial goals working on a salary for eight hours a day, unless you find a way to successfully invest disposable income. Successful people, especially those between the ages of 30 and 50, regularly work twelve to sixteen hours per day.

A TALK WITH A MATALON

Some years ago I happened to be seated on an airplane next to a member of Jamaica's renowned super-wealthy Matalon family. We chatted for the entire flight as I picked his brain, seeking to know the secrets of his family's wealth and success. He told me a story of work, hard work, working like a dog, of falling and rising again, of losing and winning again, a story of fantastic persistence even in the face of failure. For he said, it's not that you fall that is of concern; the real concern is that you rise again. After we disembarked that Air Jamaica flight, I somehow felt that the main purpose of that trip was not my geographic destination, but my mental destination. I left the airport charged up, determined to persist and succeed, no matter what my trials.

STRATEGY 4

WORK:
Going the Extra Mile

The difference between ordinary and extraordinary is that little extra. —JIMMY JOHNSON

Work, or the Methods in the DOME is where the rubber hits the road. Many plans fail because of laziness. People who work at becoming wealthy do not sleep late, watch television inordinately or work four hours per day. Neither do they use their productive time to do the groceries. They delegate what can be done by others, and concentrate on their own money-earning work.

But there is another problem with employees. Many watch the clock and do the barest minimum. Others do even less, as they turn up chronically late. They are not in the category of the man in the true story that follows. This man went the extra mile.

THE JOHN BURNS STORY

John Burns, a life insurance salesman, is a friend of mine. An Englishman, our relationship goes back to the early 70's when we met at life insurance conventions around the world. John believes in going the extra mile, of doing more than is required of him. He believes, as I do, in the mantra "Do more than you are paid for and you will be paid for more than you do." In pursuing this philosophy, John sold a very small life insurance policy to an Anglican vicar in the late 1960's. The premiums were minimal, (then equivalent to J$10 per month). Now, some insurance agents would have dismissed this small sale as no more than of nuisance value. Not so John. He lavished service on the vicar, took him to lunch, and remembered his birthday, his wife's birthday, their anniversary, and his children's hobbies. The vicar migrated to the United States and John lost contact with him for several years. In 1976, John miraculously met up with this vicar during the U.S. Bicentennial Celebrations. This is the amazing story that John told me and a group of Million Dollar Round Table life underwriters:

> "The vicar was glad to see me and said, in fact, he wanted to contact me. Since he left England, he was bequeathed a large fortune of hundreds of millions!" Then John reconstructed a part of the conversation:
>
> *Vicar:* "John, I can't forget the service you gave me, the relationship you developed with me and my family when I had no money. I don't know what to do with this fortune, but now that I am living in America, they tell me I will have to pay out a substantial amount in death taxes. Could you place an insurance policy on my life that would cover the taxes when I die?"
>
> *John:* "Vicar, I believe I can help. Let's get you medically examined!"

The commissions from this one case alone made it possible for John, should he so choose, never to work again for the rest of his life. The act of going the extra mile paid him for more than he did. For John did not really make this sale in 1976; he made it in the 1960s, when the vicar was a "small man". Many salespeople forget to service the account, failing to realise that today's "small man" can be tomorrow's Butch Stewart.

Success is in relationships, not in commissions.

If you build lasting relationships with people, if you serve them, if you help them achieve their goals, you will achieve your own. Give people what they want and you will achieve what you want. Michael Manley once told me, "You can't take a man to the mountain top without getting there yourself."

I have not seen John again since the 1980s, but I hear of him, through our mutual friends in England. I had just finished a motivational speech in Singapore where I told John's story to a group of life insurance agents. As soon as I stepped off the platform, a young, attractive Chinese lady ran up to me, her eyes sparkling. "Mr. Williamson", she said, in heavily accented English, "I have not met John Burns personally, but I am a graduate of his Trust." "What Trust?" I asked her. What she told me led me to find out that John Burns did not consume those millions upon himself. He established a foundation for underprivileged persons, and this girl from China had finished her schooling, thanks to the John Burns Trust. She then entered the life insurance industry. Was John lucky? Perhaps, but guess what? The harder you work, the luckier you get.

Strategy 5
ACHIEVE OPTIMUM PERFORMANCE IN YOUR LIFE

STRATEGY 5

How to Overcome Procrastination

Act decidedly and take the consequences.
No good is ever done by hesitation. —THOMAS HENRY HUXLEY

George Claude Lorimer, speaking about procrastination said, "Putting off an easy thing makes it harder. Putting off a hard thing makes it impossible." There is more than a grain of truth to this statement.

If you have found yourself putting off important tasks for another time, you are not alone. Procrastinators work as many hours in the day as other people do, and often work longer hours, but they invest their time in the wrong tasks. Oftentimes, they are unable to distinguish between urgent tasks, important or routine tasks, and end up doing tasks without prioritizing them.

Often procrastinators are not aware of this flaw until confronted by those closest to them.

Over my many years of corporate life, I am aware of persons whose desks are always overburdened by files, paper folders, pieces of scrap paper, or a hundred post-it notes reminding them of things to be done. However, because these persons fail to prioritise, they end up doing routine tasks at the expense of urgent or important duties. This situation is not usually a problem of procrastination in itself, but one of disorganisation as well.

Let us consider a definition of procrastination. Procrastination, as defined by the Webster's College Dictionary, is to defer action; to delay or to put off until another day or time. A friend once told me that the dictionary gurus missed out one very important aspect when defining the concept of procrastination, which is, "because you don't feel like it". However, the corporate world would not agree that my friend's definition of procrastination is applicable at the work place. What would an employee say when, upon not receiving his or her pay cheque, the boss said, "I didn't feel like writing cheques today"?

WHY DO PEOPLE PROCRASTINATE?

Procrastination and disorganisation are integrally linked. Poor time management and the inability to prioritize are key factors which contribute to "putting things off for another time." Individuals also "put things off" because they are waiting for the "right" time or the "right" mood to tackle the task at hand. Others might be bored by such tasks, might not have an understanding of what is required, or are just avoiding things which are disliked or difficult. When you procrastinate, you might be under pressure, stressed or intentionally taking time out for yourself. Whatever the reason behind procrastination, it must be dealt with and controlled before opportunities are missed, your career is derailed or worse.

Fear of the consequences or fear of the unknown is another reason behind procrastination. Those of us in the life insurance industry are well aware of the common objection to buying, "I need time to think it over." Many times the clients need the insurance but simply fear the unknown or the future. On occasions, they procrastinate because they fear the results of the mandatory HIV test. But as far as your health is concerned, the more you procrastinate, the worse might be the outcome.

In my job as a paramedic, I was doing a physical examination of a patient when I discovered a highly suspicious lump in the lady's breast.

Immediately, I referred her to the physician who directs my paramedic activities. I advised her to go to the doctor immediately, and thought that she left my location and went directly to the doctor. However, months later, much to my shock and dismay she had not gone to the doctor! By the time she got to him (under severe pressure from me) a mastectomy was the immediate and only treatment. It was cancer.

STRATEGY 5

Taking Charge of Procrastination

Procrastination is opportunity's assassin. —VICTOR KIAM

It is not the size of the tree but the depth of its roots that make it strong. Procrastination usually has very deep roots that encourage someone to approach tasks which are easier, most convenient and more to their liking. As these "comfort" tasks are being addressed, other important tasks begin to pile up. It is important to recognise that you do tend to procrastinate, and that you understand the reasons for doing so. Overcoming procrastination usually involves better organisational and time management skills. These can be learnt. Procrastination may also be an indication of a physical or psychological problem that can be treated.

Let us now look at specific ways in which we can conquer "putting things off":

- Accept that there is no magic wand. You will eventually have to do the task anyway, especially if you can't delegate the work to someone else.

- Get a simple Things To Do pad, and use it every day to write down the things you are going to do or have already done.
- Prioritise by dividing your tasks into three segments: (1) Urgent; (2) Important and (3) Routine.
- Break down tasks into manageable sets.
- Ensure that you have the right information and tools needed to complete the tasks at hand.
- As the saying goes, "Just do it!!"

Procrastination has a way of ruling our lives if we do not bring it under control. However, it may not just rule your life, it may take it.

STRATEGY 5

Managing Time Stealers

Dr. Omar Davies is a man I admire for his discipline of self-organisation. Some years ago I called him at his office. He was not in but, much to my surprise, he returned my telephone call. I thought I was someone special, since the minister of finance was returning a telephone call to me, an ordinary citizen, but not so. Several people have told me that he always returns his telephone calls. I contrast his discipline and humility to many others with far less responsibility, less workload, more time on their hands, who are either too busy or consider our calls too unimportant to make the time to return them.

Another exceptionally busy person who always returns telephone calls is Dennis Morrison, chairman and board member of several government companies, and, it seems to me, involved in everything else in Jamaica. If he can find time to return his telephone calls, why can't you? I happen to work with Dennis in the public service and am amazed at the many things he does simultaneously and with such efficacy. So I picked his brain concerning returning telephone calls. This is what he told me, "Tony, first of all it is respect. I return telephone calls because I have respect for people. That is the key. But I also make it a discipline. I will spend my afternoons returning calls. If I don't reach the person, I will try the next day. The aspect is a system. My office details all calls and ensures that I have the message in as much detail as possible. A system helps".

I also spoke with the busiest persons I know and I asked them about the management of their time. Based on what they told me, I have concluded that busy, successful persons are the ones most likely to return your calls. Prime Minister Michael Manley told me years ago, "If you want something done, find a busy [public servant] to do it."

Busy, successful people have found a way to manage time stealers. Time stealers are those things or persons who interrupt your work, who waste your time. There are several time stealers—the telephone, the drop in visitor, meetings, unnecessary paperwork, and so on. Let's deal with the telephone.

TELEPHONE SLAVERY

The telephone is an interesting thing. It is, on the one hand, one of the greatest time savers. It saves time driving to see someone; it saves meeting time. Through conferencing, it saves multiple calls by bringing many people together, thus saving huge aggregate travel time. It saves useless trips. As a salesman for many years, I saved gasoline and time by calling ahead, only to learn that my prospect (who had given me an appointment) was not there. The telephone saves letter writing/emails and the waiting they entail for a response.

Ironically, on the other hand, the telephone is one of the biggest time stealers. Nine out of ten executives spend at least one hour each day on the phone and four out of ten spend more than two hours per day.

Time management consultant R. Alex McKenzie has this to say: "A devastating factor in the battle for control over our environment is the incoming [telephone] call. In this tactical battlefield lies the shattered nerves of many a manager who conquered other, more imposing time robbers. Executives with secretarial help head inexorably down the road to defeat when they fail to give their secretaries authority in this critical area". (The Time Trap). McKenzie was of this opinion in 1972, before the advent of cell phones. What would he say today?

An interruption of one's work by the telephone has always been a problem. But with mobile phones now in proliferation, addiction to the telephone is now a major time waster that, as was famously said, you can have two, "You take out one and call yourself and you take out the other and say, 'hello, hello.'".

The problem came home very sharply to me when I was interviewing a lady who had sent in an application for a job. In the middle of the interview, her cell phone rang from the depths of her ample hand bag. She fought with the bag to find it and, having found it, she proceeded to answer the call, putting me on "hold"! I said to myself, "Anyone can forget to turn off his/her cell phone, so I'll let this pass." To my horror, the lady's phone rang again and the interviewee again interrupted the meeting to speak with her caller. That did it for me. I politely terminated the interview, said goodbye and after she left, threw her application form into the trash basket. If she spent so much time on the phone during an interview, what would she do on the job?

Successful people, be they executives, managers or housewives, recognise the tyranny of the telephone as an interruption of their work. How many executives accept phone calls in the middle of a conversation with another person in their office? I have found the situation intolerable as I have sat in one-on-one meetings with executives and (humorously) told them that I had better leave their office and then phone them, since it appears easier to get their attention on the phone than in person. Not only is this type of interruption a time stealer, it is plainly bad manners. If you give someone an appointment to see you, at least pay him, or her, the courtesy of a meeting without several phone interruptions.

MANAGING PHONE CALLS

In speaking with many busy successful executives, they employ certain strategies to manage the telephone. Here are some:

1. They have their secretaries screen calls and take messages while they are occupied with important, time sensitive work.
2. They schedule a certain time in the day to return telephone calls. Many will return calls first thing in the morning, others at set times in the day.
3. Many turn off their cell phones and schedule a time to note

voicemail. They will then return calls at a set time. Some have their secretaries keep their cell phones while in office.

4. Many people don't dial their own calls. A secretary or assistant will do that for them and connect the call.

5. Time sensitive executives limit call time. Experienced executives know that the opening words of a call will determine the length of a call. If an executive calls and starts like this, "Hi, Bill, how are you today?" He/she is setting himself up for a long reply that talks about health, family, World Cup Cricket, the latest political scandal, etc., etc. Instead, the executive may start the conversation, "Bill, I need a couple of quick answers if you have a minute." He may end the conversation, "Fine Bill, you've been a great help. See you in church on Sunday. Bye now". Many people refuse to speak for longer than three minutes while on the job. The busier you are, the more business-like the conversation.

STRATEGY 5

Taming Telephone Tyranny

Dos't thou love life? Then do not squander time, for that is the stuff life is made of. —BENJAMIN FRANKLIN

I mentioned previously that the telephone had two sides to it. It saves time, and it steals time. We are all aware of how it saves time, but few people realise how much it robs time. It is a classic time stealer. There are, however, strategies to employ to tame this tiger. Although these strategies are used by busy, successful executives, most of whom find the time to return your calls, the principle of managing the telephone extends to housewives as well. A housewife may not have someone else to answer the phone for her, but she does have voicemail at her disposal.

BUSY EXECUTIVES

A very serious challenge to executive time is the incoming telephone call. If one does not have a strategy to manage it, one will rarely get much done in the average workday. These incoming calls do not really arrange themselves into priorities. Calls come in from anyone, from anywhere. If you are some kind of public figure, it's worse.

MANAGING INCOMNG CALLS

One very successful way of preventing random telephone calls from distracting an executive, is to have a professional secretary or assistant intervene.

A secretary's first concern when she takes a call on behalf of her boss is to determine the urgency of it. Secretaries and assistants will come to realise that a significant number of incoming calls directed to the boss or manager can, in fact, be directed to and handled by someone else in the organisation.

A secretary or assistant might have a greater challenge if the caller wants information on a subject that is the manager's area of responsibility. A secretary can politely and diplomatically discover the purpose of the call and ask whether she may provide that information since she is privy to it. This, of course, presupposes that the secretary has been empowered by her boss and given the liberty to use her brain and the authority to act. So many managers hold on to information as if they were the sole repository of all facts in the organisation, and must personally deal with all matters. This is not good management.

If the caller requires information that only that particular executive can handle, the assistant must determine whether it is of sufficient urgency to warrant interrupting her boss. She may well say, "May he call you back when he is free?" If the truth be told, it is not a bad idea to have automatic call-back responses to everything but emergencies. This allows an executive the power of control, the ability to work uninterrupted until he or she has a convenient time to speak on the telephone.

A secretary can develop the skill of being helpful to both executive and caller. She can put the caller on hold and say simply, "Let me see if I can interrupt her". She then asks the executive for a quick answer that will satisfy the caller. This type of interruption can be so rapid that it is not a serious distraction to the executive, who immediately resumes her work while her assistant provides the required information for the caller. This type of collaboration between the executive and her secretary comes with practice and an understanding between executive and assistant.

RETURNING CALLS

There are tremendous advantages to managing the telephone by a call-back system. It allows the executive the time he or she needs to work without interruption, and gives the executive the option to decide which calls he or she wishes to return personally.

The grouping of calls in this manner dramatically reduces the number of interruptions. What is more, it places the executive in control of the telephone instead of the telephone controlling him. The call-back system also allows the secretary to provide the executive with the information he needs when he returns the call.

Clients will often call my office and say, "What is the cash value of my policy? Can I get a loan on it?" My secretary takes this information, researches the query and provides the answer. When I return the call, I can be specific. Often however, she will return the call, providing the information, leaving me to continue my work at hand.

OTHER STRATEGIES

Many people don't dial their own calls. A secretary or assistant will do that for them and connect the call. This saves time for the executive.

CELL PHONES

People employ different strategies with mobile phones. Some people turn them off while at work, and schedule a time to listen to voicemail. Others leave the cell phone with an assistant to take messages.

More and more people carry two or more mobile phones, usually for cost savings. But a very busy person may use one phone only for family, personal or emergency calls. When that phone rings, he answers it. The other receives voicemail which he can return at a convenient time.

LIMIT YOUR TALK TIME

Although I am addressing these remarks to executives, the limiting of call time goes for teenagers as well, many of whom suffer from telephone diarrhea, chatting incessantly on the phone when they should be studying. Housewives as well, with an unfinished To Do list, should be like time-sensitive executives who limit call time.

STRATEGY 5

Visitors, Meetings and Paper

Time wasted is existence; used it's life. —EDWARD YOUNG

George Berkwitt puts it interestingly as he describes executive life:

> What gives the manager's job a nightmarish quality are the interruptions—the constant and seemingly endless telephone calls, sudden meetings and personnel problems which seem demonically designed to run his schedule off the track.

I include in "nightmarish quality" the drop-in visitor to your office and the paper-manufacturing factory calling your desk.

MEETINGS

In my days of corporate life, there were few things that bothered me more than the seemingly endless meetings. The higher up in the organisation you moved, the more your time was spent in meetings. Sometimes it's all day, after which you return to your desk to find a pile of unfinished work. Meetings are, of course, very important. They should however be scheduled, with a starting time and an ending time. Long, open-ended meetings tend to become counterproductive by yielding diminishing returns after a certain time.

THE HIGH COST OF MEETINGS

At a seminar of twenty top managers, the cost of a meeting was calculated as follows: the average salaries were calculated (excluding fringe benefits), other expenses of the meeting were added and a calculation made as to the cost of a two hour meeting. The meeting started 30 minutes late, and the cost of those 30 minutes was $33,506 before it got underway! If companies took the time to do a cost-benefit analysis of meetings, they might be surprised at what they discover.

Since management meetings are unavoidable, here are some suggestions for effective meetings:

1. Have them at scheduled times
2. Pre-circulate the agenda
3. Start on time, end on time
4. Do not make the meeting too long
5. Summarise progress and decisions made before adjourning the meeting.

Do not forget to return telephone calls that came while you were in the meeting.

THE DROP-IN VISITOR

Many times your work is interrupted by the drop-in visitor to your office. This can be a delicate situation since you must be courteous and at the same time, block interruptions from unscheduled visitors. Most of these visitors you know quite well, some are friends. How do you handle drop-in visitors? Here are some suggestions:

1. If you have a secretary, authorise her to screen your visitors. She should have enough knowledge of your priorities to make an appointment or have the visitor see you, if she deems it urgent.
2. Go to the office of your colleague. If someone in the organisation wants to see you, you can go to that person's office or another

suitable location. By preventing a colleague taking a seat at your desk, you maintain control of your time.

3. Meet the visitor outside the office. If you are not aware of the visitor's purpose, meet him or her outside your office. If you invite the person into your office, you lose control. Be courteous and friendly to your visitor with a warm smile and friendly handshake. "How can I assist you?" You might ask. You can then control what happens depending upon the response.

4. When a visitor pops up because your secretary was away from her desk or he simply bypassed the secretary, stand up to confer with him. By standing, you prevent the visitor from sitting, thus giving yourself a psychological advantage.

Another way to use the standing position to control a visitor's time is to quietly stand when your time with a seated visitor has expired. Usually, this will send him a message that the conference has ended.

Some executives have a prearranged plan with their secretaries who will knock, come and remind the executive of his next appointment. You may then easily and confidently terminate the meeting.

PAPER

Regardless of what they tell you, there is nothing like a paperless office. I once worked with a life insurance company that, with the latest information systems, announced itself as "the paperless office". It generated more paper than even the traditional ones!

I learned a secret about managing paper from the Million Dollar Round Table. The secret is this: Touch or handle paper once, and act on it. If you cannot make an executive decision on it when you read it, either delegate the responses or place a stick-on note for follow-up at an appropriate time. Be generous with your trash bin, knowing what to discard, and what to file. Pushing paper gives you the impression of being busy, but paper-pushing is not necessarily the best use of an executive's time.

STRATEGY 5

THE 1440 CLUB:
Recognise that You're a Member

We are all members of the 1440 Club, from the moment we come into this world until the day we leave it. Man or woman, boy or girl, rich or poor, we are involuntarily members. What is the 1440 Club? The 1440 Club is the club of time. There are 1440 minutes in a day—no more, no less.

If you should ask people if they have enough time, most would say that they don't. You have heard many people sigh: "I wish I had more hours in the day." But this is the paradox of time, the enigma of the 1440 Club: few people have enough time, yet everyone has all there is. Time waits on no one. Time management consultant R. Alex McKenzie makes this observation: "Time is a unique resource. It cannot be accumulated like money or stockpiled like raw materials. We are forced to spend it, whether we choose to or not, at a fixed rate of 60 seconds for every minute. It cannot be turned on and off like a machine or replaced. It is irretrievable". *(The Time Trap).* Chaplin Tyler puts it this way: "Time is the most inexorable and inelastic element in our existence."

In Jamaica, there is a culture of lateness. If you are old enough you may remember the hilarious comedy, *Eight O' Clock Jamaica Time* in which a clock below this sign showed 8:30. We routinely turn up late to meetings, church, parties, work and almost every conceivable engagement.

Time management, of course, is far more than punctuality, but we shall begin here since that area of time management is often a symptom of a greater overall problem.

MINDSET

I once counseled a young man who was chronically late. Nothing I said to him, or what anybody else advised him, could make him arrive on time for his appointments. He just about admitted he could not change—until he migrated to New York. I went to visit him in New York, and much to my amazement, he had completely changed. He was not just on time for his engagements, he was early! What had happened to him? His wife told me quietly that the very first time he arrived late for his job in New York, by the time he arrived, someone else was in his place! That was the last time he was ever late for work—and anything else. He had a completely different mindset.

WHY YOU SHOULD MANAGE TIME

The management of time is the management of yourself. If you cannot manage time, you cannot manage yourself. If you cannot manage yourself, can you manage others with credibility? Management guru, Peter Drucker, has made the observation that unless he manages himself effectively, no amount of ability, skill, experience or knowledge will make an executive effective. And Gerald Achenbach, a former CEO of one of the most successful chains of supermarkets in America summarises his philosophy of managing time. "It's your time you're spending. You should be its master and not let it master you. You can't master time unless you're first willing to master yourself"

CHANGING YOUR MINDSET

Books are a dime a dozen in our bookstores on the practical details of managing your time—how to identify "time-stealers", and "time-savers" and so on. My purpose in writing this section is not to rehash the myriad bits of practical advice but to get you to change your mindset; to go far deeper than the practical tips. I am convinced that, unless a man changes his mind about time management, adopts a new philosophy, books on time management are about as useful to him as ice to Alaska. And this is why people go through their entire lives being late, regardless of the books, seminars, etcetera, in which they participate. They are late because of their mindset.

Teaching someone practical tips about managing time, without a mindset change, is like treating cancer with a 'bath' from a balm yard in St. Thomas. It is useless hocus-pocus, Mephistophelean mumbo jumbo, destined to fail, as surely as night follows day.

STRATEGY 5

THE 1440 CLUB: Change Your Mindset

In the previous section, I made the point that the Fourteen Forty Club is the club of time. There are 1440 minutes in a day—no more, no less. The paradox of time is that most people say they don't have enough time, but everyone has all there is—86,400 seconds in a day.

Some people learn to manage time. Others allow time to manage them. There are some in the second category who are indifferent to the consequences of their failure to manage time. These persons end up wasting time, being less efficient and losing money. Time is money.

To manage time is to manage yourself. To manage yourself means for many a change in mindset, the adoption of a new philosophy. How do you change your mindset?

INTEGRITY

The first thing to do is to see yourself as a whole person, a person of integrity. When we use the word "integrity", we usually equate it with honesty. It does involve honesty, but the word has a far broader meaning.

The word integrity comes from a Latin word INTEGRITAS which means wholeness, soundness. Wholeness speaks to the balance of systems making up the person, all of which fit together to make the complete individual. A motor car has integrity of structure when all of its parts fit together to create a smooth, rattle-free ride.

A person of integrity is trustworthy, level headed, reliable. He or she is predictable—not a loose cannon on deck. If a person of integrity gives you his word, his word can be relied upon. How does this relate to time? Here's how: If you tell me you will meet me at 8:30 a.m., then if you are a person of integrity you have given me your word. You will keep your appointment barring circumstances over which you have no control because you gave me your word. For the person of integrity, his word is his bond.

RESPECT FOR OTHERS

You will not likely be late for an appointment if your thought pattern (mindset) allows you to respect the time of the other person. For, inherent in chronic lateness is a lack of respect for the time of the other person or persons with whom you had an appointment. Is it that they have nothing to do with their time than to wait upon me? Who am I anyway that I should inconvenience another? And what about the Golden Rule: *Do unto others as you would have them do to you?* If the roles were reversed, would you like to be wasting your time, waiting upon someone who told you he or she would meet you at 6:30 p.m., only to have that person saunter in at 7:30 pm?

GOING FORWARD

The first step in moving from chronic lateness to proper time management is to make a decision. Nothing happens until a decision is made, and a decision not to decide is to decide not to. Decisions we make in our lives are responsible for where life takes us. You do not need to have the cacophony of thunder and lightning to change your mind-set. All you need is a quiet resolve, a decision to be on time for all of your engagements. After you have dealt with the mindset, consider these practical tips for managing time.

PUNCTUALITY

The big problem with many Jamaicans is punctuality. In order to conquer lateness, as a chronic problem, here is what you can do:

1. **Be conscious of time.** Most people wear a wristwatch or carry a cellphone. Check the time periodically.

2. **Leave your location earlier.** If you are going on an appointment, leave earlier than you are used to. If you live in Constant Spring and you have an appointment downtown, leave early enough to cover the vagaries of traffic. Give yourself a margin of safety, in case you encounter an unexpected delay.

3. **Call ahead.** If you realise you will arrive late for an appointment with someone, call ahead (or have someone call on your behalf) to indicate that you are running late. This one step alone indicates respect for others and people can adjust their schedule to fit your new arrival time.

4. **Evaluate your performance.** Do you remember DOME—diagnosis, objectives, methods, evaluation? The 'E' in DOME is for evaluation. After a month of your new mindset, pause to assess how successful you are at arriving on time. (Incidentally, a DOME plan is an excellent tool to correct chronic lateness).

5. **Avoid "excusitis".** Do not fall into the very common trap of making excuses for your lateness, "My wife took too long to dress, the car would not start…" and so on. Take responsibility for your actions instead of shifting the blame on traffic. Traffic is not the problem, you are. If traffic cannot change, you certainly can!

Strategy 6
MANAGE SETBACKS FOR YOUR COMEBACK

STRATEGY 6

Four Choices in Times of Trouble

Trouble is universal. It will happen to all and sundry. We have trouble in our business, trouble in our family, trouble in our marriage, trouble in our health, and so on. No one escapes. No one is wafted through life on a satin pillow. We all have rivers to cross, mountains to climb, obstacles to overcome. As Charles Dickens puts it about your life and mine, "It was the best of times, it was the worst of times." How does one manage in a time of trouble?

Dr. Robert Schuller once outlined four attitudinal philosophies and choices that you face in a time of trouble. Over the years, in my own life, I have found the knowledge of these four choices to be greatly helpful as I work my way through a problem. The four choices are: resentment, passive acceptance, inventing a solution and finally, preventing a deterioration of the problem.

Your first choice is to resent the problem. Unfortunately, this reaction is as common as it is useless. Resentment is more damaging to you than it is helpful to the solution of the problem. Resentment, not unlike stress, bitterness and ill-feelings toward anyone or any situation, will only make you worse off during your problem. If your problem is the loss of your job, the loss of a relationship, or the loss of money, do not resent it.

> *When you face loss, do not look upon what you have lost; consider what you have left. There is never a total loss, for if you have life, you have hope. Begin to plan again more intelligently and see this as opportunity to grow again; bigger, better, wiser.*

Your second choice is to simply consent to it, to act as if the problem did not exist. If you take this mental position, you are missing out on a great lesson that life is trying to teach you.

You cannot ignore the problem. Ask yourself some questions. What might I have done differently? What are the steps to take now to move forward? Who has experience to advise me and counsel me? Seek help. If your marriage is falling apart, don't give up on it or ignore it. Seek counseling from a professional.

Your third choice is to invent a solution. It has been said that every failure, every heartache, every adversity brings with it the seed of an equivalent or greater good.

You can bounce back from every ill wind, for every cloud has a silver lining. So face your problem, learn from it, and grow by it.

Your fourth choice is to prevent the problem from getting worse. Let's suppose you were recently diagnosed a diabetic. It's a waste of mental energy to curse your luck. Instead, you can obey your doctor and keep the disease from getting worse.

You can ignore it and eat all the mangoes you want—and take the consequences. Or you can change your diet and lifestyle, things that you have the power to control.

Orison Swett Marden, the inspirational writer said, "There are three types of people in the world. There are the WILLS, the WONTS and the CANTS. The first accomplish everything; the second oppose everything; the third fail in everything". My question to you is this: In the face of your current problem, in which category are you? Take a mental inventory of yourself, "a check-up from the neck up."

Life will always be a challenge. You are not alone in facing the problems of life. Ralph Waldo Emerson summed it up this way: "Nature provides the exercise, the challenges for the development of the person. All development is the result of effort, and this effort is what strengthens the person." Never give up!

STRATEGY 6

Promise, Problem, Provision

There may be no heroic connotation to the word 'persistence',
but the quality is to the character of man what carbon is to steel.
—Napoleon Hill

Most of the successful people I know today came through trials. Some suffered financial failures, others a painful divorce, some a catastrophic illness. Yet, they triumphed. It is not that successful people did not have trials for hidden trials are a phenomenon of life. No one, and I mean NO ONE, ever gets the prize without a fight; no one lives the dream without some pain; no one succeeds until he or she has endured hardship.

In life, there is a principle, and it is this: Promise, Problem, Provision.

The **Promise** is the dream—what you believe you can achieve, the wealth you want to acquire, and the position of leadership you feel is yours. But life is a curious amalgam of opposites, a balancing act of action and reaction.

Every Promise brings with it a **Problem.** Truth be told, on the journey to success, the most important aspect of the journey is the Problem. It is in the fires of testing and trials that one's character is fashioned. As we move towards power, fame and fortune, we are not really qualified to assume the mantle of greatness until we have been humbled in the valley of adversity.

Unless you solve the Problem, there is no **Provision.**

The principle of success enshrined in Promise, Problem, Provision is as old as the Bible. The classic story is of Joseph, the dreamer. In the book of Genesis we see a remarkable unfolding of his life guided by Promise, Problem, Provision. Joseph had a dream, a vision about his future greatness. In his case, it was a literal dream. In your case, it might be a vision of what you want to be, do and have. But no sooner than Joseph received his Promise, he faced a Problem: his brothers were jealous over him and sold him into slavery in Egypt. But his Problem was just the beginning. Falsely accused, he was cast into prison where he languished for years. But in the darkness of adversity, he did not give up his dream. He held on to his vision. His Provision came when, miraculously, he was made prime minister of Egypt and saved that country from economic calamity.

The interesting thing I have learned from Joseph and his experience is the same which I have learned from other successful people. It is that you grow and develop character in adversity, not in prosperity. What is more, if you do not manage adversity, learn from it, grow through it, and gain mental strength from it, you almost certainly will not arrive at the Provision. Persistence through pain brings provision and power. In the valley of suffering, in the fires of trial is where you really grow in life. Being wealthy does not tell you anything about the character of a man. What he went through to achieve that wealth is more instructive. Prosperity conceals character, adversity reveals it.

Your adversity is not a weapon to destroy you, but an opportunity to strengthen you. Don't curse the darkness; light a candle. If you are going through hardship now, grow through it, be strengthened by it. Seek help if you need it, but rise above it. If a mountain faces you, climb over it, go around it, or tunnel under it. Fight, fight, fight! Even a dead fish can swim downstream. It takes muscles, courage and determination to swim against the current. But only when you have done that will you ever come into life's Provision for you. Barack Obama now faces his Problem. How he handles it will determine his Provision.

STRATEGY 6

When Trouble Comes

Even when confronted with a hopeless situation,
you still have a chance to make life meaningful…
in turning personal tragedy into a triumph or by
transforming your predicament to an accomplishment.
—VIKTOR E. FRANKYl

Charles Dickens in his novel, *A Tale of Two Cities*, expresses the contrasts of life. He wrote:

> It was the best of times, it was the worst of times, it was the age of wisdom, it was the age of foolishness, it was the epoch of belief, it was the epoch of incredulity, it was the season of Light, it was the season of Darkness, it was the spring of hope, it was the winter of despair, we had everything before us, we had nothing before us, we were all going direct to heaven, we were all going direct the other way…

When one is privileged to live a long time, one sees life for what it is. Life can be simultaneously, "the best of times" and "the worst of times". Life is a curious balance of opposites—bitter and sweet, night and day, feast and famine, health and sickness, success and failure, life and death. There is no way to pass through life without your share of problems. You and I will always have problems, and the sooner we accept that fact, the better prepared we will be, not only to face our challenges but to grow through them, and by them.

The interesting thing about life's problems is that they are like the wind that blows. The same wind that blows a ship to the north, can also take another ship to the south. It is the set of the sail that matters, not the direction of the wind. The set of the sail speaks to attitude; your attitude to what happens to you in life. The real issue of life is not what happens to you, for many things that happen cannot be controlled by you. It is how you react to what happens to you that is really important.

Take, for example, Jamaica's experience in the 1970's. This country experienced a number of challenges in its economy at that time. Real estate values fell precipitously as people sold their houses and emigrated out of fear. People with cash bought Cherry Gardens' mansions for pennies on the dollar. Today these houses are worth tens of millions.

While the hotel/tourism industry was languishing, a young salesman of appliances named Butch Stewart saw an opportunity where others saw none. Butch started to purchase these near-abandoned hotel properties in the early 1980's, and the rest, as they say, is history. The same wind that drove many to migrate from Jamaica into the "greener grass" of North America (and into hardship and marginalization for many) blew Butch into wealth and riches.

Another young salesman, R. Danny Williams, envisioned a dream he was determined to fulfill. He wanted to create a local insurance industry in which Jamaicans would be employed, an industry that would invest in Jamaica and enhance the development of our country. He started Life of Jamaica from scratch, an outgrowth of the emerging nationalism of the 1960s.

Life of Jamaica went on to make a fortune for Danny Williams, but trouble came. During the financial meltdown of the 1990's, Danny Williams watched helplessly as his fortune diminished before his eyes. He lost a staggering amount of the value of his shares—an experience that would have caused some men to jump from a tall building. But Williams continued to believe in his dream. He never gave up. Life of Jamaica (now Sagicor Jamaica) was reorganised and today stands like a colossus with assets running into the billions. What if he had given up?

You too might be facing your own problems, and you too will experience life as "the best of times, the worst of times." How you conduct yourself during the worst of times speaks volumes about your character. You can be a better person, a wiser investor, a stronger individual because of the worst of times.

STRATEGY 6

Your Results Define Who You Are

What you do speaks so loud I cannot hear what you say. —RALPH WALDO EMERSON

The older I become, the more I watch what people do, and the less I listen to what they say. Talk is cheap, and some of the greatest underachievers in life are some of the greatest talkers. One reason not to take politicians seriously on the campaign trail is that they are full of promises, desiring to be given the reins of power. But how many of them follow through on their promises? This is not just a Jamaican phenomenon; it exists all over the world.

But results are the most important clue to your success or failure in life. What you do brings results. What you say is meaningless without corresponding action and results. Why are things not working out for so many people? Jack Canfield has this to say; "The easiest, fastest and best way to find out what is or isn't working is to pay attention to the results you are currently producing. You are either rich or you are not. You either command respect or you don't. You are either maintaining your ideal body weight or you are not. You are either happy or you are not. You either have what you want or you don't. It's that simple. Results don't lie!"

STOPPING EXCUSITIS AND THE BLAME GAME

If you wish to move ahead in life, you have to stop making excuses and blaming others. If you are a salesman and behind in your quota, do not blame the company. The fault is yours.

If you are overweight, do not blame genetics or make excuses. Change your lifestyle by eating right and getting regular exercise. It takes discipline.

Are you unhappy in your job? You are the one who took the job. You are the one who is staying in the job. Not reaching your goals? You are the one who gave up on your dreams. As the old Negro spiritual says, "Not my mother, not my father, but it's me, O Lord."

Quit blaming others. Wayne Dyer puts it succinctly, "All blame is a waste of time. No matter how much fault you find with another, and regardless of how much you blame him, it will not change you."

GIVE UP COMPLAINING

Lou Holtz, a successful coach said, "The man who complains about the way the ball bounces is likely the one who dropped it". When you complain about something, you are admitting that something better exists. If you complain about your income you are admitting that there is better income available out there. If you complain about your house, you know there are better houses out there. If you complain about your job, you are admitting that there are better jobs available.

But guess what? Many who complain are unwilling to take the risks associated with changing what they are complaining about. But you cannot get to second base without taking your foot off first. If you are not prepared to take the risk of change, then quit complaining. The circumstances people complain about are, by their very nature, things that can be changed. You can get a better job, make more money, lose weight, eat healthier food, live in a nicer house or move to a better neighbourhood. Fear is the reason many do not make these changes. The fear of failure allows us to rationalise in our minds that complaining is better than risk taking.

Don't just sit there and complain. Do something. Lead, follow or get out of the way. What you do is what you get.

STRATEGY 6

The Hidden Benefits of Failure

We are continuously faced by great opportunities brilliantly disguised as insoluble problems. —LEE IACOCCA

The language of the Chinese carries an interesting word. The word that means "danger" also means "opportunity". The word is like a coin. One side is "danger", but the flipside is opportunity. In this linguistic feature, Chinese is not unlike Hebrew, the language of the Jewish people, for Hebrew carries within many of its words explicit and hidden meanings, and phonetics which bear the sound of the thing the word describes. One can actually gain an insight into the culture and psyche of a people by studying their language. In the word for danger, the Chinese are saying, "Turn it around and make it opportunity". Let us examine the relationship between these two meanings in the same word.

As laypersons, we would view few things more filled with risk and danger than brain or open heart surgery. One slip of the scalpel and.... But herein lies the paradoxical opportunity. People need heart and brain surgery, and the men and women who will seize the opportunity to become cardiac and neurosurgeons end up as multi-millionaires. The higher the risk, the greater the returns! The greater the danger, the better the opportunity! It is all a matter of perspective.

IS THE GLASS HALF FULL, OR IS IT HALF EMPTY?

Are you like the shoe salesman who, when sent to a far country to sell shoes returned dejected saying, "There is no opportunity to sell shoes there. The people all walk barefooted." Or are you like the next salesman whom the company posted there and who sent back a telegram: "Send all the shoes you can. Opportunity limitless. The people here have no shoes as yet."

STRATEGY 6

Wilma Rudolf

Wilma Rudolf was born in Tennessee in 1940. Her left leg was shorter than her right, and she grew up with a limp. In fact, cruelly, they nicknamed her "Limpy." At age four she contracted both scarlet fever and double pneumonia. Confined to a wheelchair, doctors informed her mother that it would be necessary to massage her paralyzed leg every day if there was to be any hope of its usefulness. Over the next two years her mother and family members took turns to daily massage her leg and to drive her frequently on a ninety-mile journey for heat and water therapy.

At eight years of age, she was fitted with a leg brace and was the butt of jokes at school. In the face of constant teasing and mocking she remained determined, remembering her mother's words of encouragement to her. Her mother had always pointed her vision past her disability, and made her know that she could achieve whatever she deeply desired and worked hard at.

As she grew up, she realised she loved sports and she played rough and tumble with her nineteen siblings, refusing to be limited by her disability. At age eleven, she discarded her leg brace and never used it again. She loved basketball and was also excellent in track and field. She ran for her high school and did so well at sixteen, Limpy made the US Olympic team, winning a bronze medal in the 400-metre relay in 1956.

Four years later, Limpy ran in the AAU Championships where she ran 22.9 seconds for the 200 metres, a world record then. When Limpy was chosen for the Rome Olympics, one of the USA's leading newspapers criticised her coach (later to become a USA coach for the women's track team), saying that Coach Ed Temple was not fit to be a coach. He was attempting to embarrass America by "choosing a cripple as one of its representatives, a symbol of man's inhumanity to man".

But Wilma Rudolf went to Rome. The crowd went wild as this limping black girl scorched the 100 meter track for a gold medal. But more was to come, because Rudolf was entered by her coach in the 200 metres race. She was to compete against Jutta Heine, Germany's speed demon over the 200 metres. "On your marks" said the starter. "Set." The starter's gun shattered the deathly silence at the beginning of the race, and as they say, the rest is history. Rudolf 'limped' to her second gold medal, for she remembered her mother's words, "you can achieve greatness, if you trust God and believe in yourself."

The circumstances of her physical body should not have allowed her to enter much less win two gold medals. Her limp should not have made her win at Rome, but then, the laws of aerodynamics say that a bee is not supposed to fly. Its body is not made to fly, but it flies anyway because they forgot to tell the bee it was not aerodynamically made to fly.

Wilma was not yet through. She entered the mile relay. She was anchoring the relay but a faulty baton change placed Jutta Hein ahead of her. As she got the baton she thought of her mother, she thought of her country, and she looked to her God. Then, not unlike the race in which Sherone Simpson ran down Marion Jones, Limpy ran down and passed Jutta Heine, winning her third gold medal! As she stood on the raised platform to the strains of the Star Spangled Banner, she thought of her mother. She told reporters later that her mother gave her the belief that she could live above her circumstances and rise to greatness.

Circumstances can be a bane or blessing. It all depends on the set of your mind's sail. Do not blame circumstances for your life's misfortunes. Take responsibility for yourself and say like Winston Churchill, "Things don't happen to me; but I happen to things."

Strategy 7
DEAL WITH YOUR PAST

STRATEGY 7

Getting Past Your Past

Yesterday is a cancelled cheque; tomorrow is a promissory note; today is the only cash you have—so spend it wisely. —KAY LYONS

You may well be one of millions of persons who are not fulfilling their true potential in life because they are weighed down mentally, crippled by the memory of their past. Adversities of peoples' past lives include a failed marriage, a history of substance abuse, criminal activity, a failed business venture or bankruptcy, failures in academic pursuits, children who have not turned out well, and a host of other mistakes, failure and bad experiences. How can one move on and achieve success with a past that seems to cloud one's vision and sap one's creative energy?

Everyone in life has a past, but most of us will have a future. A critical success factor in life is the mental acknowledgement that the past is passed, gone forever, irretrievably lost. You cannot turn back the hands of the clock. You cannot go back into the past and undo what has already been done. Dwelling on the past is a futile exercise and a waste of precious mental energy. You need to accept this fact and think about your present circumstances and your future. In going forward, here are five steps to take for a brighter tomorrow:

1. Analyse, but don't dwell on, your past failures, and identify the lessons that you need to learn from these experiences. Failure

and adversity are the greatest universities of life. It has been said that anyone who does not learn from his past mistakes is condemned to repeat them. Failure is not the end of the story. Failure is only the opportunity to begin again more intelligently.

2. Forgive yourself. In the next section on "Forgiveness", one thing that I should have highlighted but did not is the absolute necessity to forgive yourself. Sometimes it is easier to forgive others than to forgive ourselves, but the same capacity to forgive others must allow us to forgive ourselves and to put the past behind us. A wise person said, "Forgiveness does not change the past but it does enlarge the future."   And forgiveness is a decision, not an emotion.

3. Change your behavior. Two of the most important ideas I get from Albert Einstein are: (i) If you continue to do the same things and expect different results, that's the definition of insanity, and (ii) The significant problems we face cannot be solved by the same level of thinking that created them. Ultimately what is really important is not what you think or what you say, it's what you do. You can change the way you speak to people— use kinder words, be less critical. You can study more diligently, spend money more thoughtfully and save more consistently. If gambling wasted your money, quit gambling. If alcohol is restricting your potential, quit drinking. Seek help if you need to, but make the change.

4. Set a goal. Goal setting can change your life and erase past failure by giving you astonishing success. But goal setting is different from wishful thinking. Goal setting has to be specific, written down, carry time horizons and be evaluated regularly. If, for example, you would like to be financially independent or wealthy in five years, it is a waste of time merely to say, "I want to be rich". Instead, write down the exact amount of money you intend to have by 4:00 p.m. Wednesday December 31, 2017. Then write down the goods and services you intend to exchange for this money, for there is no free lunch. Find out the people

who can help you, the obstacles you will have to hurdle and the hours you will have to spend to accumulate this sum of money.

5. Invest your money. When you have surplus money, decide where you can invest it so that when you are not working it will be working for you. If your investments do not keep up with inflation, you are on a financial treadmill. Wealthy people find ways to invest their money so that their returns exceed inflation.

Finally, rule out failure. Regardless of your past, get past it by a powerful mental decision that you should affirm aloud daily, "I will not fail, but succeed at this venture." Specify the venture, believe you will achieve it and act as if it is a done deal.

STRATEGY 7

The Importance of Forgiveness

When I refuse to forgive, I am burning a bridge that someday I will need to pass over. —JOHN MCDOWELL

When I was a little boy, I remember hearing someone say the following in response to a wrong done to her: "I will never forgive him until the last nail rattles over my head in the coffin". As a young boy, I did not fully comprehend the seriousness of what she was saying, but instinctively, I knew something was drastically wrong with a statement like that. It spilled vitriol, venom and vexation of spirit. Why would someone want to die with unforgivingness in his or her heart? Later on in life, of course, I came to understand the shattering significance of such a statement, a statement that said "I hate you so intensely I will be ushered into eternity with this hate against you". Then, what does this mean for you?

Apparently, some people, like old John who was dying, have a slightly different take on forgiveness and death. Old John was on his deathbed, and with time running out, he wanted to make things right with his friend Sammy. Although they were best friends, during recent times their friendship had soured and they were at odds with each other. In fact, in the last few months they had not spoken to each other at all. Not wanting to die with matters unresolved, John sent for Sammy.

When Sammy arrived at John's hospital bed, John apologised for the part he played in damaging their friendship. John said he was afraid of entering eternity with animosity and bad feelings between them and he wanted to make things right before he died. Then John reached out for Sammy's hand and said, "I forgive you Sammy. Would you please forgive me?" Sammy was moved to tears and he also quickly forgave John. Just as Sammy was leaving, however, old John shouted after him: "But remember, if I don't die and somehow get better, this doesn't count!"

Forgiveness, however, is not just about your death. Forgiveness has everything to do with your life. To forgive is to set aside a hurt or wrong done to you, to treat it as if it never occurred, to release the person who offended you and let him or her off the hook. Bitterness and internal anger can have both psychological and physical side effects. Bitterness creates tension within; tension creates stress. Stress may result in a vast array of maladies—from insomnia to ulcers, from high blood pressure to stroke, from mental anguish to dementia.

Unforgivingness is like a great stone tied to your back, a crushing weight that you carry around with you everywhere you go, while the offender walks free as a bird, as light as a feather.

During the 1970s, my friend, the late Rev. Derek Prince, told a group of us a remarkable story of an encounter with a woman who had come to him for prayer. The woman was afflicted so badly with an arthritic hand that she could barely move her fingers which were curled up into a ball. During the conversation with the woman, Rev. Prince realised she was carrying a deep-seated hatred of her father. I reconstruct the conversation between Rev. Prince and the arthritic lady:

> Prince: "You must forgive your father".
> Woman: "I cannot forgive him"
> Prince: "You have to release your father. Go and tell him you forgive him".
> Woman: "I cannot do that. I cannot forgive him".
> Prince: "Why can't you forgive him?"
> Woman: "Because he is dead".

Rev. Prince told the lady that the forgiveness was not for the benefit of her deceased father, but for her own benefit. She should go to his grave, speak over the tombstone and say, "Father, I forgive you for all the hurt you caused me". The woman obeyed and the moment she forgave her father, she was healed of her arthritis—no further need for prayer.

If this story is true and I believe it is, could forgiveness be an act of enlightened self-interest?

STRATEGY 7

FORGIVENESS: Decision Not Emotion

Forgiveness does not change the past,
but it does enlarge the future. —PAUL BOESE

If you are going around in life carrying hurts and offences against you, you are living in bondage. You must shed this harmful baggage by forgiving those who have wronged you. Forgiveness is more for the benefit of the one who does the forgiving, not the one who is forgiven.

FORGIVE AND FORGET

People often say, "I can forgive, but I cannot forget". But many people who say that are described by Henry Ward Beecher: "I can forgive, but I cannot forget is only another way of saying, I cannot forgive." Whether you agree with the statement or not, multiplied thousands of people are walking around remembering and recalling their hurts and with those painful memories, failing to forgive their offenders.

DECISION NOT EMOTION

People often make the mistake of confusing forgiveness with forgetting the wrong done to them. To forgive and to forget are not the same. Forgiveness is a decision. Your memory is an emotion. It is a neurological impossibility to forget those things done to you that caused you pain. The important thing here is not to dwell on the memory which you cannot control. What you can control are your actions, your spoken words, and your reaction to the offender.

A very important mechanism of forgiveness is decision. Decision and not emotion drives the forgiving process. If you were to wait until your emotions were no longer painful, you would hardly ever forgive anyone. But although we as human beings are emotional creatures, we are primarily decision makers. Usually, emotions will line up after we have taken the decision, not before. Let me illustrate how decision, not emotion works in forgiving someone—even your worst enemy.

Suppose you borrowed some money from me. You gave me an I.O.U. note evidencing the loan I gave you. For some reason, you are not able to repay me. I can do one of two things. I can take legal action against you or I can forgive the debt. If I chose the latter, I simply tear up the I.O.U. and throw it into the trash can. I may not feel good about the fact that you have not repaid me. My emotions might be painful, but I chose to forgive you your debt by making a decision, a decision to tear up the I.O.U.

Forgiveness is to tear-up the I.O.U. that you are holding for your offender. It has nothing to do with emotion. It is a decision. At the time you decide to forgive, you may still be hurting at the wrong done to you. But usually, after the decision is made, emotions line up to support the decision. Your decisions drive your life. If emotions rule your life you are living on a dangerous roller coaster.

HOW LINCOLN TORE UP AN I.O.U.

Abraham Lincoln was a young, struggling lawyer when he was asked to do a particular high profile case. The other attorneys on the case were well known, well-established legal luminaries. One of these attorneys, on seeing

Lincoln, remarked, "What is that gawky ape doing here? I refuse to work with him. Get rid of him." Lincoln remained unperturbed and acted as if he did not hear the insult. As the case progressed, Lincoln was treated as an outcast by the other attorneys. They never recognised his presence. But Lincoln was keenly observing the trial and listened intently to his insulter's masterly handling of the case. He won the case easily. The next day Lincoln was quoted as saying, "His brilliant argument was a revelation to me. He was expertly prepared, fluent in his presentation, and undoubtedly the most professional questioning I have ever seen. I can't hold a candle to his abilities. I am going to have to study law all over again".

Years later, Abraham Lincoln became president of the United States and that same attorney who had rudely insulted him became his most outspoken critic. However, Lincoln never forgot the man's brilliance in court. When Lincoln needed to make an appointment for secretary of war, he chose Edwin M. Stanton, the very man who had cruelly wounded and insulted him. In doing this, Lincoln tore up the I.O.U. and held no lifelong grudge against his detractor.

Shortly afterwards, Lincoln's life was tragically cut short by an assassin's bullet. Stanton was inconsolable, grief stricken and sobbed, "Now he belongs to the ages."

Do you have an I.O.U. that you need to tear up? Do it now before you "belong to the ages".

Strategy 8
HARNESS THE POWER OF PERSISTENCE TO PERSEVERE

STRATEGY 8

The Courage to Continue

Tribulation brings about perseverance, and perseverance, proven character; and proven character, hope.
—THE HOLY BIBLE, ROMANS 5:3-5

Time magazine in an article commented on the quality of success that enables a man or woman to persist despite the odds, to fall and rise again, to outlast failure and to end in victory. The writer said, "What ultimately defines us is not what happens to us but how we deal with what happens to us". If you are ever to be a success, to be outstanding in your field, you must be persistent.

Jack Canfield puts it this way: "Persistence is probably the single most common quality of high achievers. They simply refuse to give up. The longer you hang in there, the greater the chance that something will happen in your favour. No matter how hard it seems, the longer you persist, the more likely your success."

Persistency of purpose is power. Dogged determination determines destiny. True greatness always embodies a never-say-die spirit, the unflappable and stoic determination to see failure as only another opportunity to begin again, more intelligently. Persistence is all powerful. It was Napoleon Hill who wrote, "There may be no heroic connotation to the word 'persistence', but the quality is to the character of man what carbon is to steel".

Do you sometimes feel like giving up when they bypass you yet again for that promotion, when your grades keep falling below what is required, when your marriage is on the rocks, your children are causing you sleepless nights, your husband cannot quit drinking, and all around you seems to be coming apart?

Do you feel like quitting?

Well, don't, for a winner never quits and a quitter never wins.

Life will always be a challenge. You are not alone in the difficulties you face, the disappointments you experience, the failures, the foibles, the weaknesses. We all face these things, for life is a curious amalgam of bitter and sweet, adversity and opportunity, a valley of tears and a mountain of joy. The universe is a confluence of great balancing antagonists, of inherent tensions between good and evil, day and night, feast and famine. These are not the important things. What is important is your attitude, how you respond to these outcomes, how you endure tribulation.

It was B. C. Forbes, the founder of Forbes magazine who said, "History has demonstrated that the most notable winners usually encountered heart-breaking obstacles before they triumphed. They won because they refused to become discouraged by their defeats".

There has never been a successful or famous person who has never known failure or has not had to overcome staggering odds:

- John Milton wrote *Paradise Lost* while totally blind.
- Beethoven composed his greatest music while totally deaf.
- Being sightless did not prevent Ray Charles from achieving greatness.
- After years of battering around searching for meaningful employment which he could not find, a man called Albert Einstein wrote his seminal Theory of Special Relativity while working as a clerk in a patent office.
- It took Noah Webster thirty-six years to complete *Webster's Dictionary*

- It is said that Ernest Hem ingway reviewed the manuscript for *The Old Man and the Sea* eighty times before submitting it for publication.

In another famous example, a man loved drawing comic strips as a boy, but as a young man he was advised by an editor in Kansas City to give up drawing. Kicked out, he walked the streets. He kept knocking on doors. He persevered until finally a church hired him to draw publicity material. He worked out of a little garage and had for his only company a little mouse he befriended. He drew a sketch of this mouse and called him Mickey.

His name? Walt Disney! And his rodent friend? Mickey Mouse!

When he approached the bank about doing a project with Mickey Mouse, they threw him out, laughing him to scorn. But in 1931, with a nervous breakdown, rejections and setbacks, Disney persisted with his dream. The rest is history.

One of the ultimate examples of persistence, is Abraham Lincoln. History regards him as perhaps the greatest president of the United States, but few people know how he got into the White House. Here is his story:

- 1832 - Lost his job. That same year he ran for a seat in the Legislature and was severely defeated.
- 1833 – Went into business and went broke.
- 1833 – Ran for Speaker of the House and lost.
- 1843 – Ran for a seat in Congress and lost.
- 1849 – Applied for a job with the US government and was turned down. That same year he applied for life insurance and was declined.
- 1854 – Tried for the US Senate and lost.
- 1856 – Tried for nomination for Vice President of the USA, but was roundly defeated.
- 1858 – Tried again for the US Senate and lost again.
- 1860 – Elected President of the United States of America.

As Sir Winston Churchill so aptly puts it: "Never give in! Never, never, never!!"

STRATEGY 8

Persisting in the Face of Failure

Fall down seven times, get up eight times.
—JAPANESE PROVERB

We often hear about people who have failed. In the great financial meltdown in Jamaica during the 90s, many businesses went belly-up; many captains of industry lost their iconic status. Some, unable to take the embarrassment of financial failure, fled the country, or worse. There are some, however, who endured the hardships, who weathered the storm, who fell and got up again, rising from the ashes of defeat like the Phoenix of old. You learn more about successful people, not by what they are today, but by the failures they endured to get there.

You know a man's character, not when he is on the mountain top, but when he is in the valley. Adversity reveals character. Prosperity conceals it. You can tell how a person will handle himself at the top when you see how he handles himself at the bottom. The powerful place may bring arrogance and pride in the one who has never been in the powerless place. But then again, some people forget that they were once in the powerless place and become arrogant, disrespectful and haughty in the powerful place. And life, the great leveler of men, brings them back down to their knees to learn again that true greatness lies in humility.

Failure in itself is not a bad thing. What is important is what you learn from having failed. Nineteenth century English bard, John Keats said: "Failure is, in a sense, the highway to success inasmuch as every discovery of what is false, leads us to seek earnestly after what is true, and every fresh experience points out some form of error which we shall afterwards carefully avoid."

What some people consider disaster is the breakthrough opportunity they needed. I have heard people say: "The best thing that happened to me is when I got fired." I have also seen ladies, having wiped the tears from their eyes after a bitter divorce, rise to heights of great achievement. They themselves admit that such achievement might have been impossible without the fires of suffering that strengthened their will to succeed. Failure in their marriage became success in their lives.

Failure can teach you far more than success. In fact, if you have never failed, you might not be able to handle fame and success. Super-salesman Herb True says of failure: "Successful people often experience more failures than failures do. But they manage to press on." Real estate magnate and millionaire, Robert Allen adds, "One good failure can teach you more about success than four years at the best university.

Failing might be the best thing that ever happened to you."

I have repeated many times in my articles that it is not what happens to you that is important. What ultimately defines you is how you handle what happens to you. You cannot judge a man, nor take the measure of a man by his failures—until you know how he handled them. The key for people who fail is found in what Confucius said, "A man is great not because he hasn't failed; a man is great because failure hasn't stopped him."

Thomas Watson, the legendary IBM founder, was asked what the secret of success was. He quickly replied, "Double your failure rate." In other words, expose yourself to more risk; go to the batting crease more often, fall down seven times, but get up eight times.

Sir Gary Sobers, the greatest cricketing all-rounder of all time, and the greatest batsman of my generation, made more "ducks" than you would think. But he still ended his career with a batting average among the all-time greats. Why? He took more risks. He went to the crease many, many times, swung his bat and hit more than he missed. He persisted. Your most spectacular failure or your deepest disappointment may ultimately prove to be your best teacher and greatest blessing. Do not despise your failures. Look for what they can teach you.

STRATEGY 8

The Power of Persistence

Nothing in the world can take the place of persistence. Talent will not; nothing is more common than unsuccessful individuals with talent. Genius will not; unrewarded genius is almost a proverb. Education will not; the world is full of educated derelicts. Persistence and determination alone are omnipotent. —CALVIN COOLIDGE

During World War II, England was staring down the barrel of the Nazi gun. She was on the verge of being overrun by the Hitler war machine. Bombs were falling everywhere. People were dying, fires were raging and supplies were dwindling. Only a narrow body of water, the English Channel, stood between England and the ferocious hordes of Nazi Germany.

Sir Winston Churchill became known as the great wartime prime minister of England because his brilliant oratorical skills motivated a beleaguered England to persist to the end.

In speaking to the House of Commons of the Parliament of the United Kingdom on June 4, 1940, Churchill encapsulated the British resistance against Hitler with these words:

> We shall go on to the end, we shall fight in France, we shall fight on the seas and oceans, we shall fight with growing confidence and growing strength in the air, we shall defend our Island, whatever the cost may be, we shall fight on the beaches, we shall fight on the landing grounds, we shall fight

in the fields and in the streets, we shall fight in the hills; we shall never surrender …

And as they say, "The rest is history." Against all odds, England went on, with its allies, to defeat Hitler. And herein lies a great truth in life. The winner is not necessarily the one who starts with a flourish, but the one who persists to the end.

If you should ask me what I have found as a common feature of the lives of the many successful people I have studied, it is persistence. The will to continue, the deep desire to keep striving toward that goal, the ability to pick yourself up, dust yourself off and start all over again. For true success has everything to do with how you rise up from that fall. We all will fall, but not all rise up again.

If you speak with successful men and women in Jamaica today, the Butch Stewarts, the Douglas Oranes, the Audrey Hinchcliffes, the Matalons, the Issas, the Danny Williams's the Oliver Jones's, the Bev Lopez's, the hundreds of other successful people and captains of industry, you will find one common thread running throughout their careers; they fell and rose again. They faced tremendous obstacles, but overcame them. They endured deep disappointments, but they persisted. You see them driving around today in their SUV's and BMWs, and one is tempted to say, 'They were born with a silver spoon in their mouths.' But this is more often than not quite untrue. They endured hardships, failures, bankruptcies, embarrassment, ridicule and discouragement, but they persisted, and like cream, rose to the top.

Sometimes the best way to succeed is simply to endure, to persist, to last. You will learn that a winner never quits and a quitter never wins.

Johann von Goethe sums it up well. He said:

There are but two roads that lead to an important goal and to the doing of great things: strength and perseverance. Strength is the lot of but few privileged men; but austere perseverance, harsh and continuous, may be employed by the smallest of us and rarely fails in its purpose, for its silent power grows irresistibly greater with time.

Take courage, my friend. Hang in there and outlast your troubles.

STRATEGY 8

Code of Persistence

Herman Sherman lists eight ingredients of persistence. They are:

1. I will never give up so long as I know I am right.
2. I will believe that all things will work out for me if I hang on until the end.
3. I will be courageous and undismayed in the face of odds.
4. I will not permit anyone to intimidate me or deter me from my goals.
5. I will fight to overcome all physical handicaps and setbacks.
6. I will try again and again, and yet again, to accomplish what I desire.
7. I will take new faith and resolution from the knowledge that all successful men and women have had to fight defeat and adversity.
8. I will never surrender to discouragement or despair, no matter what obstacles may confront me.

Jacob A. Riis, a Danish immigrant who became a prominent social reformer in the 19th Century, said something profoundly true:

> When nothing seems to help, I go and look at a stonecutter hammering away at his rock, perhaps a hundred times without so much as a crack showing in it. Yet, at the hundred and first blow, it will split in two, and I know it was not that blow that did it, but all that had gone before.

Riis has focused on one aspect of success that often eludes us—persistence. For, if you examine his analogy with the stonecutter, you will see yourself there, and you might have a better understanding of why some things do not work out for you in life. You hammer at your rock—your goal—and stop just short of the rock splitting in two, not realizing that all your efforts gone before were working for you to achieve success. Because you could not see it, you did not believe it. But achieving success demands faith, a belief that what you are doing WILL work out for you, even though you cannot now see the results.

If you are to fulfill your dreams, Sherman's Code of Persistence must drive you.

Shakespeare said, "We are such stuff as dreams are made on."

Read the biographies of successful men and women, consider the stories of our own Jamaican heroes; Audrey Hinchcliffe, Butch Stewart, Robert Levy, Danny Williams, Merlene Ottey, George Headley, Usain Bolt. History rings with stories of people who believed in their dreams and persisted until those dreams became reality. And if you read Barack Obama's book The Audacity of Hope, you will begin to understand the monumental achievement of a black man who becomes the president of the United States. It all started as hope. Then it moved to faith, then to work and dogged persistence in the face of seemingly insurmountable odds.

- Success calls for tireless persistence:
- Plato labored over his Republic masterpiece. He rewrote the first sentence nine different times before he was satisfied.
- Beethoven lost his hearing BEFORE he composed many of his great symphonies for which he is famous.
- John Milton wrote Paradise Lost while totally blind, rising at 4:00 a.m. to fashion this epic.
- Franklyn D. Roosevelt was struck down by polio, but he persevered. From a wheelchair, he led the free world as president of the United States.

- Adam Clarke labored forty years writing his commentary on the Bible, while Roger Gibbon took twenty-six years to complete the Decline and Fall of the Roman Empire.

These people all persisted, for they understood Eleanor Roosevelt's words, "The future belongs to those who believe in the beauty of their dreams".

Never give up!

Strategy 9
LEARN FROM THE HORSE'S MOUTH

STRATEGY 9

Redemption Song

What is the difference between an obstacle and an opportunity? It is our attitude toward it. Every opportunity has a difficulty, and every difficulty has an opportunity. —J. SIDLOW BAXTER

My wife and I are not frequent movie goers, but we like a good movie. We have contrasting tastes however, in movies. She likes the romantic and the "My Fair Lady" types of stories; I like action—the "Rambo" type of movies. Over the years we have come to an agreement about the cinema. I will accompany her to her type of movies—and sleep through them. She will accompany me to my type of movies—and endure them.

One day she suggested that we go to see a movie called Seabiscuit. I groaned inwardly, and was not too willing to go. But she prevailed upon me. When I heard that this movie was about a race horse, I knew I would be sleeping through it. So at the start of the movie, I settled in to sleep. Unfortunately, I had drunk a large amount of diet coke, and the caffeine in it kept me from sleeping, so I was forced to watch. To my amazement, the movie, which is a true story, turned out to be one of the greatest movies I had ever watched.

The movie is the story of a discarded race horse of the 1930s, rejected, abused, and written off as useless; yet goes on to become arguably the greatest racehorse of the 20th century. It is also the story of the redemption of four lives:

1. A millionaire who had suffered deep sorrow in the tragic death of his son and the break-up of his marriage, and how his life is redeemed through owning Seabiscuit.

2. It's the story of an eccentric trainer living in poverty and the edge of society in the Great Depression in America. He restores his life by training Seabiscuit. He utters one of the memorable lines in the movie, "You don't throw away a life just because it's banged up a little."

3. The movie is also the story of a half-blind boxer turned jockey, a life in ruins that is redeemed and restored by a loving relationship with Seabiscuit.

4. Finally, it is the story of Seabiscuit himself, sentenced never to win a race, and yet who becomes one of the greatest horses ever to grace a race track.

The movie is a painting of life and its lessons, a clear demonstration that no life is beyond redemption, no situation too hopeless, and no disaster that does not carry within it the seed of a corresponding greater good. Over the next chapters in this section, I shall outline the lessons from Seabiscuit, the story of redemption. There are seven lessons as follows:

1. Physical limitations, adversity and hardship are no indication of your true potential. Your true treasure is your mind, not your circumstances.

2. Every one of us is uniquely gifted in something. It does not matter that we may have been abused, discarded and "left for dead". If we find that "something" with which our Creator has endowed us, we can rise and soar into the skies of success, leaving our past behind us.

3. Words have power. The things you say can either heal or hurt. What you say to yourself (your thought life), what you say to

your children, to others, is important. Words are often a self-fulfilling prophecy.

4. To achieve extraordinary success, one must engage in extraordinary work. The training that Seabiscuit had to endure to beat the then Number One horse—a magnificent, unbeaten stallion called War Admiral—was phenomenal. There is no free lunch.

5. You can use adversity to make you better, not bitter. True growth of character takes place during the fire of trials and adversity.

6. Confronting your fears, dealing with them and leaving them behind, is important for your life. Fear can cripple and disable you, keeping you from achieving your deepest dreams.

7. It is darkest just before the dawn. Many times the worst things happen to you before the best things happen to you. Always maintain in your thinking, "The best is yet to come."

If these lessons can work for a horse, then surely they can work for you!

STRATEGY 9

Overcoming Discouragement

If you have never seen the movie *Seabiscuit,* I strongly urge you to buy or rent the DVD, sit back and watch some of the greatest lessons of life. This particular version of the movie *Seabiscuit* was directed by Gary Ross and stars Tobey Maguire, Jeff Bridges and Chris Cooper.

Truth be told, these persons are not the true stars. The real star, the true hero is a "broken down racehorse", discarded as a hopeless loser, cursed, abused and sold to millionaire Charles Howard for a rock bottom price. At the end of the movie, Seabiscuit's jockey summarised this remarkable true story, "We found a broken down racehorse and thought we would fix him. But in a real sense, he fixed us." The ownership of this small, unlikely hero of a horse was to redeem and restore the life of a very discouraged man, a millionaire who had tragically lost his young son, and who suffered the breakup of his marriage.

The loving relationship with this horse also took his jockey, Johnny "Red" Pollard, out of deep discouragement from the hand that life had dealt him, for he was abandoned by his parents and left in the Great Depression to fend for himself.

Seabiscuit "fixed" the life of his eccentric trainer, Tom Smith, a man who was living on the edge of poverty but whose love of horses was the turning point in the life of Seabiscuit. His entry into the story line was at the point where they were about to destroy another racehorse because it was lame.

He intervened and begged them to spare the life of that horse, "What good would that do?" they asked. "He's lame, he will never run again."

Then Tom uttered what was for me the most memorable line of the movie, a line what would eventually preserve the career of the injured jockey and possibly saved the life of Seabiscuit when he tore a ligament. He said, "You don't throw away a whole life just because it's banged up a little."

The redemption of Seabiscuit's own life is an example to illustrate that one can come back from defeat, rise from the ashes of failure to achieve greatness. Life dealt Seabiscuit a cruel hand as a young horse. He was beaten, abused, cursed, and thought to be useless. The way the young horse was treated affected his mind. He became discouraged, bitter and angry. No one had shown him love except his mother, from whom he was snatched as a foal. By the time Charles Howard bought him, he was useless and no good—or so his previous owner thought. Until his new trainer befriended him, his new jockey loved him, and his new owner cared for him.

Remarkably, as the trainer and jockey began to speak words of kindness to him, ceased whipping him and began to tell him that he was a good horse, a hidden power within Seabiscuit began to emerge. The curse of discouragement that covered him like a shroud began to lift, and the horse began to believe in himself and to relate to the kindness that was being shown to him for the first time in his life.

I have had to counsel scores of persons over my lifetime. People come to me on the verge of suicide, in the depth of despair. Some are bitter, many are angry. The most common problem I unearth during these sessions is the emotional and psychological damage done to these people as children. Many were brutally beaten by savage parents, but strangely, the physical beatings are not the problem. It's the verbal abuse that scarred them, parents who told them they were dunces, idiots, worthless, that they would amount to nothing.

Verbal and emotional abuse of children can scar them for life. Abuse of children of any kind is abominable, but it may surprise you how powerful an effect verbal abuse has. If it can negatively affect an animal, imagine what it can do to a young, impressionable child. Bless your children. Do not curse them. When Seabiscuit began to be blessed with words of encouragement and love, he changed into the hidden champion he was born to be. We shall see, as his story unfolds, how this horse was to put his past behind him and rise to the top.

STRATEGY 9

The Dark Times of Your Life

A man of character finds special attractiveness in difficulty, since it is only by coming to grips with difficulty that he can realise his potentialities.—CHARLES DE GAULLE

We all have potential hidden within us. Once, a little boy stood with his mother and stared at a magnificent carving of a statue by Michelangelo. After his mother explained that the statue was made from marble, the little boy asked her, "Mummy, how did Michelangelo know the man was in there?" The boy's innocent question is telling. It takes a lot of cutting, chopping, and changing to reveal what is inside of you. Can you imagine the hammering that the marble had to endure in order to reveal the statue?

And so it is with us. Life may hammer us. Circumstances may beat us down. Things may go against us. But if we persevere, something precious and worthwhile will emerge from our trials.

In the movie *Seabiscuit*, a true story about the life of a rejected horse that became the greatest racehorse of the 20th century, there are several lessons to be learned. The story shows that if a horse can turn his life around, so can we all. No life is beyond redemption, no situation too hopeless; no difficulty or adversity that does not carry a potential benefit.

In the story of Seabiscuit, the horse began to win races after a string of defeats and failures. With loving care, expert guidance and training,

Seabiscuit began to show his true colours, his potential that was always there.

At the time Seabiscuit was winning races, there was a magnificent, unbeaten stallion called War Admiral. War Admiral, the prized possession of a millionaire, was much larger and stronger than Seabiscuit. He had never been defeated and, apparently, could not be defeated. Seabiscuit's handlers challenged War Admiral's owner to a two-horse race. Although the offer was rejected at first as being ridiculous, popular pressure was brought to bear on War Admiral's owner, and he finally agreed to the race.

Seabiscuit's trainer realised that no horse could ever catch up with War Admiral if the latter horse jumped ahead at the start. So the trainer decided to teach Seabiscuit to jump out first; how he accomplished this can be seen in the movie. The point of interest to me is that the trainer decided to keep his plans away from the press by training Seabiscuit in total darkness—at the dead of night. Seabiscuit's jockey was blind in one eye and was not able to see well in the day much less at night. During one of the runs in total darkness the jockey complained, "I can't see." But the trainer uttered another incredible line in the movie; "Don't worry about that. He can see."

And so it is with your life and mine. There is many a situation that we go through which we can't see, understand or immediately explain. But a Higher Power is seeing for us and carrying us through. There are so many situations that we look back to and see that even in our disappointment, in what we thought was failure, things worked out for good.

Many times in our lives we cannot immediately see the purpose in our suffering. But later on as life unfolds, we find that there was a purpose to our trials, that we are now stronger, wiser. Brokenness carries a purpose and it is said that bones grow stronger at the places where they are broken.

It is important to know what our Creator can see when we can't see, that when we saw only one set of footprints in the sand that those were the times He carried us on life's journey. Seabiscuit's extraordinary night training was to lead him to his greatest victory, but he had yet one major hurdle to overcome, a hurdle that you too may have to deal with.

STRATEGY 9

Your Best is Yet to Come

The man who wins may have been counted out several times but he didn't hear the referee. —H.E. JANSEN

The big day arrived for Seabiscuit. The Pimlico racetrack was filled to capacity. Thousands were allowed inside the track to stand, joining the thousands seated in the stands. This was the race of the century, a two-horse race between the powerful, unbeaten War Admiral and the small maverick Seabiscuit. America shut down for the event. Offices were closed, people sat in groups and listened to radios.

Seabiscuit was to be ridden by another jockey since his jockey 'Red' Pollard had suffered an accident and was hospitalised. Pollard gave the new jockey some advice. He told the new rider that Seabiscuit would jump first and would initially lead. But at a certain point in the race he should restrain Seabiscuit and let War Admiral catch up with him. He explained to the jockey that Seabiscuit had an extraordinary competitive spirit. If Seabiscuit was able to look into the eyes of any opponent, that generated a turbo drive that would rocket him ahead of any horse whose eyes made contact with his.

The race began and Seabiscuit jumped first and was leading War Admiral. Then the jockey eased him up and the feared War Admiral came beside him. They ran head to head, a fantastic piece of cinematography. Then Seabiscuit looked into the eyes of the feared, mighty War Admiral. And the rest is history. Seabiscuit took off like a rocket and this rejected, unknown, small apology for a racehorse rose up to overthrow the king of the track, the feared War Admiral. America went wild.

But what is the lesson here? Confronting your fears! Fear often cripples and disables.

Seabiscuit looked War Admiral straight in the eye, and left him behind. You too must confront your fears, look them in the eye and leave them behind you. Confront and leave behind you the fear of failure, the fear of rejection, the fear of people. Race ahead in life to the greatness to which you were called, leaving your fears behind you.

This victory by Seabiscuit was not the highpoint of his career. Not long after winning this race, tragedy struck. He suffered a life threatening injury to his foot and, according to the vet, would never race again. The vet offered to "put him down" for owner Charles Howard.

Howard refused and answered, "You don't throw away a life just because it's banged up a little."

Seabiscuit's life was spared, and what was described as a disadvantage to him and was part of the reason for his earlier rejection, became his ally and saviour. Seabiscuit was small and light. He did not have the traditional weight of the average, successful racehorse. So over time, with less weight to contend with, his leg healed, much to the surprise of the experts.

And here's the lesson: Often what seems a disadvantage in your life can become your greatest strength over time. Physical limitations and adverse circumstances are not necessarily meaningful limitations. Accept yourself for who you are, maximise your strengths and turn lemons into lemonade.

Seabiscuit not only recovered from a life threatening injury, defying the odds, but went on to win his greatest races after his darkest moment. And so it is with life. It is darkest just before the dawn. The best things of your life often happen after the worst things of your life. People who thought it was all over when their house burned down, when they suffered a heart attack, when they endured a painful divorce, often rise up after that to experience the best of times from the worst of times.

STRATEGY 9

Finding Your Gift

...but David encouraged himself in the Lord his God.
—THE HOLY BIBLE, 1 SAMUEL 30:6

The early life of the racehorse Seabiscuit was one of failure, abuse and discouragement. He overcame discouragement because he was surrounded by persons who loved him and spoke words of kindness to him. This changed the horse and helped to transform him from a broken-down reject to the greatest racehorse of the 20th century.

Seabiscuit had greatness in him all along. He just did not know it. So have you.

You are not destined to fail. You were born a winner and the sky is the limit. Your present circumstances might be as discouraging as ever. You may be broke, in ill-health, facing a divorce, made redundant, betrayed by a friend, criticised unjustly, or a host of other negatives. But these are external circumstances. They do not define you. You have to project yourself outside of the crippling confines of your present distress and into the success for which you were born.

Discouragement is the constant companion of all men. Life can deal you a bitter hand, causing you discouragement. Here are some examples of events that can drive you to discouragement:

- You may have been an employee who invested all your energy to do a work assignment, but instead of being congratulated you were greeted with railing criticism.
- A couple may be anticipating the arrival of their new born and after months of planning and preparation, they are faced with a miscarriage or a stillbirth.
- You might have worked hard, saved your money to ensure your financial stability. You then put your hard earned capital into business and due to the economy, or a host of other factors, you find yourself staring bankruptcy in the face.

These examples, and a thousand others, can lead to discouragement. If you do not deal with your disappointment positively, there are at least two reactions that you might have. At one end is anger. You are angry at people, angry at your spouse, angry with yourself. Or you might go into depression, the end point of which could be thoughts of suicide. I am frankly amazed at the number of emails I get from people contemplating suicide. Suicide is not an option, for as Vince Lombardi says, "a quitter never wins and a winner never quits". While there is life there is hope.

WHAT TO DO

- Surround yourself with people who can help you.
- Seek professional help if you are gripped by depression.
- Seek out people who have passed through discouragement and come through stronger.

Seabiscuit's change began to take place when three men surrounded him with love and attention.

They stopped beating him.

They spoke words of encouragement to him.

They loved him.

Amazingly, the horse began to change, to be less angry, and to believe in himself. For they told him (and he must have somehow understood them) that he had greatness within him, regardless of his past experiences.

And so do you.

There is a divine spark of greatness in us all. If we find it, we find a treasure that money cannot buy. Discouragement is common to all. Sometimes we become discouraged because we have failed at something. But failing at something does not make you a failure, for every heartache, every failure, every adversity carries within it the seed of a corresponding greater good.

Talking with caring people helps. But what if you are alone? Then talk to yourself. Recount your blessings aloud. You may surprise yourself at how many blessings are yours right now, despite the difficulties you face. If you are a person of faith, then do what King David did when he was running for his life and facing disappointment and discouragement from every quarter. The Bible records, "David encouraged himself in the Lord his God." Prayer changes things, and when your friends abandon you, and others accuse you falsely, your faith will keep you from inconsolable despair.

You are going to fall in life. Falling and failure are a part of life.

"The steps of a good man", the Bible says, "are ordered by the Lord and he delighteth in his way. THOUGH HE FALL, he shall not be utterly cast down for the Lord upholdeth him with His hand."

Les Brown, the motivational speaker says when you fall, fall on your back, for if you can look up, you can get up. Abraham Lincoln said, "I am not concerned that you have fallen. I am concerned that you arise."

Summary

SUMMARY

Your Master Keys to Success

Nature gave men two ends—one to sit on, and one to think with. Ever since then, man's success or failure has been dependent on the one he used most. —GEORGE R. KIRKPATRICK

Destiny is not a matter of chance but a matter of choice.
—William Jennings Bryan

Belief in oneself is a prerequisite for high achievement. Faith brings into being what is not yet seen by our natural eyes, and faith is the springboard from which one can launch oneself into great endeavours. But having established the need for self-confidence, are there any defined steps that one could take to achieve success in any venture? The answer is "absolutely", and I shall wrap up the nine strategies or master keys to success in this way:

1. DESIRE (Set the Stage for Your Success)

The first master key is desire, not just a wish or a hope, but a burning, consuming desire to achieve your goals. Many of my readers email me and indicate, "I just don't have the motivation, the desire. Can you help me?" And sadly I have to reply, "I can't. If you don't have the desire, I am not sure even God will help you, for motivation to succeed must come from your own desires, your thoughts, your mind". God will not push a man where he has no desire to go. Desire, then, must be your first driver.

2. VISION (Dream)

Most of us know the Scripture which says, "Where there is no vision, the people perish". Vision can be defined several ways. Vision is the ability to see things not as they are now but as you want them to be. Vision is also the ability to project yourself mentally outside of the crippling confines of your present circumstances into a glorious tomorrow.

Vision does not concentrate on the immediate, it sees the ultimate. Vision is also defined as solving tomorrow's problems today. An example of this is the Mona Heights housing scheme. When those houses were built, many people were critical of them, saying they were too small. But the Matalons looked way down the road and saw a vision of a need for housing solutions near the university campus. This is today's problem. They solved it decades ago.

A critical element of vision is to actually imagine yourself in possession of the thing you desire before you actually receive it. The brain is a marvelous gift. If you believe a thing strongly enough, it materialises in your life. This is the action of the Reticular Activating System (RAS) of your brain, the small section that, like a computer, receives thought impulses and programmes you relentlessly to achieve your dominant thoughts. "As a man thinketh, so is he".

Many years ago, as a young insurance agent, I heard a talk that changed my life. The speaker said that if you could believe something strongly enough, repeat it out aloud, place it on 4 x 5 cards and internalise it daily, it would be yours. He said, "Act as if you are already in possession of your desire, and it will come to you."

At the time I was driving a nine-year old Ford Zephyr Six. I however, wanted a Mercedes Benz. So I began to think it, dream it, speak it and "own" it in my mind. I was also specific that it must be air conditioned, so at times I would roll up the windows of my Zephyr to imagine air conditioning, and then roll them back down. The desire was so strong that inevitably I got the Mercedes, air conditioned as well. Mind you, a tremendous amount of hard work was what produced it, but the motivation to work hard was the dream. If you can dream it and believe it, it will be yours, for as Napoleon Hill said, "Whatever the mind can conceive and believe it can achieve."

The dream alone will not by itself produce the desired thing. Between the dream and the reality are other steps, one of which is very hard work.

3. GOALS (Create a Foolproof Plan to Succeed)

Someone rightly said, "A man without a goal is like a ship without a rudder." If you do not have goals, you drift aimlessly like flotsam and jetsam upon life's turbulent seas. "Goals serve as a stimulus in life," says an anonymous quotation. "They tend to tap the deeper resources and draw out life at its best. Where there are no goals, neither will there be any significant accomplishments. There will only be existence." John F. Kennedy put it succinctly, "Efforts and courage are not enough without purpose and direction."

What are your goals in life? What do you want to be, to do, to have? You can take a giant step in achieving your goals if you observe the following:

- **Write down your goals on paper.** There is a chemistry that positively affects people when they marshal their thoughts and take the time to write them down. In outlining your goals, set time periods for their fulfillment. Be specific. Do not say, "I want my own home". Instead, write down the type of house, the location, the size and the specific date by which you intend to have it.

- **Indicate the price you will pay for achieving your goals.** There is no free lunch. There are things you will have to do, people you will have to meet, and obstacles you will have to overcome in order to achieve your goals. Write these all down.

- **Break down your large goals into smaller portions.** This concept is understood by the well-known question and answer, "How do you eat an elephant?" Answer, "One bite at a time.
  - Focus on your daily requirements. If you are a salesperson with a company quota for the year, break your quota down into what is required monthly, weekly and daily and concentrate on the daily requirement.
  - Focusing on the immediate will eventually bring you to your larger goal. Let me illustrate: A group of soldiers were commanded to walk across a vast expanse of snow in Siberia in order to reach a certain destination. As the group marched, looking out at the vast expanse of white snow they became disoriented, and got lost. The second group of soldiers were told to do the same march. This time, however, the commander told them, "Do not look out at the vastness of the snow, look at each step you take. Take one step at a time and focus on it." The second group made it across by focusing on one step at a time
  - The 'one step at a time', 'one day at a time' principle can help you too. No matter how thorny the problem, how difficult the challenge, start where you are and take one step at a time. If you wish to unravel a knot hopelessly wrapped up in a ball, start with the single end that's visible and work your way from that single end of cord until the knot is unraveled. One step at a time
- Reduce your goals to writing on 4 x 5 cards, read them daily aloud, especially last thing at night. Repetition programs your subconscious and it is the subconscious that will drive you to the achievement of your goals. Paul Myer of Success Motivation Institute says, "What you ardently desire, sincerely believe in, vividly imagine, enthusiastically act on, must inevitably come to pass.

4. WORK (Work Your Plan, Reach Your Highest Potential)

The common denominator of all success lies in forming the habit of doing things that failures don't like to do. -ALBERT GREY

The single most important element of the fulfillment of any dream, the achievement of any goal, is work. True success is achieved not by the wishbone but by the backbone. Dreams and goals simply envisioned without the corresponding work on your part is an exercise in futility—useless day dreaming. . Many great plans end up on the scrap heap of failure because the necessary work was not applied to these plans. History is full of the cluttered wreckage of lives who wished, but failed to work; who planned, but failed to execute.

Someone said, "Vision without action is a daydream. Action without vision is a nightmare". There is tremendous significance in these words, for they are the two most important aspects of success as it relates to work. You can have all the vision you want; you can dream until dreams become your master. You will achieve nothing unless these dreams and visions are brought into reality through the medium of work—very hard work. But the quotation is useful in another sense when it says, "Action without vision is a nightmare". To put it another way, "working without a plan is futile".

Work, and hard work, is very important. But here's the issue. Simply expending calories or enduring long hours will not bring success without a plan. Work of itself will not necessarily fulfill your dreams unless you work intelligently, unless you work towards a specific goal, unless you bring the knowledge which comes from study to your work.

The great motivator, Napoleon Hill in his classic: Think and Grow Rich, refers to "specialised knowledge" as essential to success. He says, "There are two kinds of knowledge. One is general; the other is specialised. General knowledge, no matter how great in quantity or variety it may be, is of little use in the accumulation of money."

What is Hill saying? He is making the point of the absolute necessity to become thoroughly knowledgeable about your specific area of work. This means that study of your area of engagement is required. If you are a salesperson, it is not only important that you put in the hours on the road; you must also know your product and be able to answer all the questions from customers. So, intelligent work involves developing expertise in a particular area, and then working like a dog in that specialised area.

Now, having established the fact that you must develop expertise by study, let me now turn to the hours you should spend working.

THE 40-HOUR WORK WEEK

One of the biggest mistakes that people make is to believe in what has been popularised as the "Nine to Five" job. In my over forty years in the work place, I have never seen anyone accumulate financial independence by working forty hours per week. Most people who work forty hours per week will never make it. In these cases you simply work for the tax man, the utility bills and for basic existence.

The successful people in our country—and you talk to anyone of them—will tell you that it took 12, 14, 16 hours per day of very hard work to reach where they are today. If you are in business on your own, you will know what I am talking about. Entrepreneurs do not watch the clock. They finish their work. The people who live for five o'clock and who, after that, do no work to improve themselves, are destined for a street called "Average". If you work as an employee in an eight-hour a day job, find something else to do in addition to your regular job in order to improve your financial situation. Bake cakes, sell clothing or teach extra lessons.

Over the years, I have also come to see that with extra work has come beautiful compensations. I tell young people, "Do more than you are paid for, and you will be paid for more than you do." You will often find that the people who get promoted are those who will go the extra mile. I have known secretaries who worked way beyond the call of duty, doing more than they were paid for. When the breaks came, they got them, some rising to senior management and heads of divisions. Were they lucky? Well, the harder you work, the luckier you get.

5. MANAGE TIME (Achieve Optimum Performance in Your Life)

Don't say you don't have enough time.
You have exactly the same number of hours per day
that were given to Helen Keller, Pasteur, Michelangelo,
Mother Teresa, Leonardo da Vinci, Thomas Jefferson,
and Albert Einstein. —H. JACKSON BROWN JR.

We live in a different world from these quoted historical luminaries. Our world today is marked by a host of distractions such as the Internet, e-mail, telephone and television. As a result we are bombarded with information—some are useful and some are not. It is easy to get side-tracked and procrastinate from our primary tasks.

Time stealers are all around us, not only from electronics and media, but in unnecessary meetings, visitors and attending to paperwork. Now more than ever, it is important to manage or monitor our time so we perform at our optimal best. Remember, we all have the same 24 hours or 1440 minutes in any given day. How we use it is up to us. We can waste it or we can focus on what needs to get done and reach for our destiny.

6. OVERCOME OBSTACLES (Manage Setbacks for Your Comeback)

The Road of life twists and turns and
no two directions are ever the same.
Yet our lessons come from the journey,
not the destination. —DON WILLIAMS JR.

We hear the lament all the time, "Life isn't a bed of roses". It is true, but we can view obstacles and challenges in life as an opportunity for us to learn and grow.

Obstacles can occur in a variety of ways: (i) Some are beyond our control (external) such as natural disasters, the economy or even a physical limitation; (ii) Some are internal such as dealing with debt or divorce, unemployment or family issues; and (iii) Some are inherent—such as self-sabotage, procrastination, perfectionism, fear of failure, fear of success and other personality flaws that stand in the way of your success.

In whatever form your obstacles appear, the preceding chapters offer solutions to stage your successful comeback.

7. YOUR PAST IS HISTORY (Deal with Your Past)

Everyone has a past. Do you constantly harp on what could have been? Are you storing old hurts and holding grudges? How you deal with your past may well determine your failure or success in life. Remember, forgiving is more for your benefit than it is for the offender.

8. PERSISTENCE (Harness the Power of Persistence to Persevere)

I am not concerned that you have fallen.
I am concerned that you arise. —ABRAHAM LINCOLN

Great works are performed not by strength
but by perseverance. —SAMUEL JOHNSON

The next key, persistence and perseverance, is the refusal to give up even in the face of the most daunting odds. Persistence and perseverance are so important that if you do not understand and practise these principles, you will probably not achieve your goals. Inspirational writer Dr. Richard Kimbro says, "Without [persistence] you can never fully enjoy riches of any kind—spiritual or material. With this principle, others will stand and view your efforts and accomplishments with awe".

Persistence is the essential characteristic that is necessary to achieve greatness. Added to the other master keys it will inevitably lead to success. Many people give up just before they achieve success.

Persist, persist, persist.

Persevere, persevere, persevere.

Never give up.

Calvin Coolidge had this to say about persistence:

> Nothing in the world can take the place of persistence. Talent will not; nothing is more common than unsuccessful men with talent. Genius will not; unrewarded genius is almost a proverb. Education will not; the

world is full of educated derelicts. Persistence and determination alone are omnipotent.

Persistence means purpose, conviction, an unwavering belief that you will succeed eventually. It means courage, enthusiasm, a "never-say-die" attitude. It means, above all, never giving up and never giving in. No great achievement comes easily. Life is a curious amalgam of bitter and sweet, of tragedy and triumph, of victory and defeat. Life will sift out the weak, the lazy, the unmotivated, and will hand its prize to the determined, the one who says, "If it's going to be, it's up to me. I will not give up".

Sir Winston Churchill had trouble at school. He took three years getting through eighth grade because he had trouble learning English. Yet he went on to become one of the great orators of the day. Harrow School in the UK invited him to address the students on October 29, 1941, and Churchill arrived in his usual top hat, with his cigar and cane. As Churchill approached the podium the crowd rose to applaud him. He stood with poise and dignity before his learned audience. Taking off his top hat and carefully placing it on the podium beside him, he removed his cigar and looked intently at the waiting audience. Then, with a stentorian voice he bellowed, "Never give in".

Several seconds passed before he thundered again, "Never give in! Never, never, never!" There was a deafening silence as he reached for his top hat and cigar, took his cane and lumbered off the platform.

This was no doubt the shortest commencement address ever given, but to war-battered Britain, it was one of the greatest speeches ever made. The myth of Churchill only saying "Never give in" was just that—a myth. In fact, Churchill made a complete speech that included these words, but the thunderous "Never give in" made such an impact that the part became the whole in peoples' memories.

Whenever you are tempted to quit in the face of trials and tribulation, remember Churchill's words: "Never give in!"

9. LESSONS LEARNED (from the racehorse, Seabiscuit)

The movie, *Seabiscuit*, sums up all that I have discussed in this book. If a horse can turn his life around, so can we. Despite insurmountable obstacles we can still succeed. The lessons from Seabiscuit are that your best is yet to come. Don't give up, even if you have suffered tragedy. If you suffer catastrophic loss in your life, do not look upon what you have lost; look upon what you have left. If you have the will to overcome, if you display courage in the face of trials, your best is yet to come.

AUTHOR'S NOTE

Dear Reader,

Thank you for reading this book, and I hope these nine strategies will empower you to take charge of your life. The Courage to Conquer begins with your mindset. Success starts in the mind. This is the stage that you must prepare.

Once your mind is primed, you must plant the dream. Nothing happens without a dream. A bold vision for your life is the single most important thing you can do to begin the journey to success. But dreams without action will never materialise. This calls for goal-setting so you can implement that dream. Implement means doing—otherwise known as WORK. Even though you may work hard, you may fail many times but you must persevere. There may be many obstacles in your path which you must overcome in order to realise that dream. Some of these obstacles are deeply embedded in your psyche from your past. I hope this book has enabled you to come to terms with your past so you can embrace your life ahead.

Finally, everyone can be a teacher of life's invaluable lessons—even a horse. I hope the lessons I've shared about Seabiscuit will inspire you, and allow you to recognise your own gifts so that you too can have the Courage to Conquer.

Be bold, overcome any obstacle and forge your fantastic future!

—Tony Williamson
Email me at: info@tonywilliamson.org
Or visit: www.tonywilliamson.org

ABOUT THE AUTHOR

D. Anthony Williamson, popularly known as 'Tony' is a versatile achiever. He is an honours graduate of the University of the West Indies and holds a master's degree in Theology (Magna Cum Laude) from the International Seminary in Florida. He is a linguist and former professional simultaneous interpreter (Spanish/English), having trained at the Language Training Institute of the Ministry of the Public Service, Jamaica.

Tony spent more than forty years in the financial services field, rising from sales producer to president and CEO of two separate life insurance companies. Further, he achieved the distinction of being, for over forty consecutive years, a member of the illustrious Million Dollar Round Table (MDRT). This is in fact, the record in the Caribbean as he is the longest sitting member in the history of the MDRT in the Caribbean region. He has two Court of the Table and two Top of the Table memberships to his credit.

He is also an inductee in "The Hall of Fame" of the Caribbean Association of Insurance and Financial Advisors (CARAIFA), an elite group of high achievers in the life insurance industry in this region.

His career has been multifaceted. He was a two-term president of the Guild of Graduates of the University of the West Indies and a recipient of the Chancellor Hall Outstanding Lions Award. He has been a founding vice president of the Translators and Interpreters Association of Jamaica and deputy chairman of the Airports Authority of Jamaica for twelve years. An outstanding motivational speaker, who has addressed audiences across the globe with his powerful motivational speeches, he was the first West Indian to be a speaker at the Annual Meeting of the MDRT.

Tony, a 'Man of Letters' also became, later in life, a 'Man of Science' for he is today a professional paramedic to the level of Advanced Cardiac Life Support (ACLS). He also holds a certificate in Electrocardiography.

He has been a newspaper columnist on the subject of health and his popular motivational column, "Dollar For Your Thoughts" with *The Gleaner* has received worldwide acclaim.

Tony is an author, photographer, philanthropist, theologian and, in general, a counsellor and public servant. He serves as the Honourary Consul General for the Republic of Uruguay in Jamaica and is also a lay magistrate (Justice of the Peace).

ACKNOWLEDGEMENTS

In 2006 I called Dr. the Hon. Oliver Clarke, chairman of The Gleaner Company Limited and informed him of my desire to write a motivational column for *The Gleaner*. A more gracious and urbane gentleman I have yet to find. He readily agreed and referred me to the editor-in-chief, Mr. Garfield Grandison. I could not have asked for a more warm and willing reception. My thanks are due to both of these gentlemen, and to The Gleaner Company Limited that has allowed me to compile these articles for this book.

This work emanates from forty years of personal observation, studying the lives of successful men and women, and I thank them all for blazing a trail for us to follow.

My very deep sense of gratitude goes to the following people who, in ways some do not really know, were the architects behind this effort.

To Herbert "Herbie" Hall of (then) Life of Jamaica, who mentored me and taught me so much about management.

To Adrian Foreman and Danny Williams, former presidents of Life of Jamaica, whose brilliance at leading us was only matched by their compassion in helping us.

To Ray Murphy, a man of unimpeachable integrity, my friend and colleague who took me under his wings in 1976, rescuing me from the consequences of a desperate financial mistake I had made and who told me about the racehorse Seabiscuit.

To Bishop Dr. Peter Morgan, for his spiritual counsel, compassion and caring, especially during the dark periods of my life.

To Paul "Pablo" Miller, for his unconditional love, support and encouragement over the last fifty-five years.

To Winston Bennett, Tony Falloon, Frank Harrison and Frank Gordon, who encouraged me and critiqued my columns.

To Ian Boyne who, through his television programme Profile and through his newspaper articles on me, brought me to national attention and kept an interest in me throughout my career and whose many interviews on television with people who have risen from failure to success have encouraged me.

To Professor Brendan Bain, Dr. Hafeezul Mohammed, Dr. Bob Parchment, Dr. Michael O'Reggio and Dr. Winsome Segree who have either kept me alive through their brilliant work with my long standing health challenges or were my tutors in the paramedic field.

To Dr. Barry Wade, for giving me the opportunity to serve as assistant in the Mona Baptist Health Clinic, where I saw the poor, the marginalised, the sick—some of whom transformed themselves and moved from the valley and shadow of death to the mountaintop of success.

To my friend and mentor, the Hon. Danny Williams, who took the time to read the manuscript and pointed out factual errors which I was able to correct.

To the memory of my colleagues now transitioned—Eddie Yap Chung (my recruiting manager), Ossie Lannaman, Molo Walker, Clarence Denny, Dickie Sampson, Owen Thompson, Wes Parker, Trevor Barnes, Keith McFarlane, Adalbert Alleyne, Neil Jones, Conrad Levy, Ken Hawley, John Sutherland, Jean Gordon-Somers and Alvin Alexander.

To Bruce Etherington, one of the greatest financial advisors alive, a mentor of mine.

To Guy Baker, past President of the Million Dollar Round Table, for his friendship, love and wise counsel.

To Johnne Syverson, for his unfailing support during my trials of life.

To my children, Caroline, Paul and Craig, for making parenting a joy and not a sorrow.

To my wife Jean, for her loving, inspirational support.

To my editors Michelle Neita and Lena Rose for their impressive level of professionalism.

To my executive assistant of many years, Yvette Love, for her indefatigable typing and retyping of the manuscript.

Finally, to my Lord and Saviour Jesus Christ, whose I am and whom I serve.

BIBLIOGRAPHY

Bettger, Frank. *How I Multiplied My Income and Happiness in Selling.* New Jersey: Prentice-Hall, Inc., 1982

Brown, Les. *Live Your Dreams.* New York: William Morrow and Company, Inc., 1992.

Brussell, Eugene E. *Webster's New World Dictionary of Quotable Definitions.* New Jersey: Prentice Hall, 1988, 1970.

Canfield, Jack. *How to Get From Where You Are to Where You Want to Be.* Great Britain: Harper Collins Publishers, 2005.

Collins, Jim. *Good to Great.* USA: Harper Collins Publishers Inc., 2001.

Drucker, Peter F. *The Effective Executive.* London: Heinemann Professional Publishing Ltd., 1967.

Great Quotations, Inc. *Motivational Quotes.* Illinois, 1984.

Hill, Napoleon. *Think and Grow Rich!* USA: Aventine Press, 2004.

Hill, Napoleon. *Success Through A Positive Mental Attitude.* New York: Pocket Books, 1960.

Kimbro, Dennis, Napoleon Hill. *Think and Grow Rich, A Black Choice.* New York: Fawcett Columbine, 1991.

King Jr., Rev. Dr. Martin Luther. *Strength to Love.* Cleveland, Ohio: First Fortress Press, 1981.

Lakein, Alan. *How To Get Control Of Your Time And Your Life.* USA: New American Library, 1974.

Mackenzie R. Alec. *The Time Trap, Managing Your Way Out.* USA: AMACOM, 1972.

Schwartz, David J. *The Magic of Thinking Big.* New York: Cornerstone Library, 1975.

Spinrad, Leonard and Thelma. *Speaker's Lifetime Library.* New York: Parker Publishing Company, Inc., 1983.

The Holy Bible.

Timberlake, Lewis. *Born to Win.* Wheaton, Illinois: Tyndale House Publishers, Inc., 1986.

Wikipedia the free encyclopaedia. *Winston Churchill's Speeches.*

www.ingramcontent.com/pod-product-compliance
Lightning Source LLC
Chambersburg PA
CBHW071201160426
43196CB00011B/2160